THE OFFICIAL
WEDNESDAY
COOKBOOK

THE OFFICIAL
WEDNESDAY
COOKBOOK

The Woefully Weird Recipes of NEVERMORE ACADEMY

* ◦ * ◦ * ◦ * ◦ * ◦ * ◦ * ◦ * ◦ * ◦ * ◦ * ◦ * ◦ * ◦ * ◦ * ◦ * ◦ *

Mari Mancusi with recipes by **Jarrett Melendez**

* ◦ * ◦ * ◦ * ◦ * ◦ * ◦ * ◦ * ◦ * ◦ * ◦ * ◦ * ◦ * ◦ * ◦ * ◦ * ◦ *

Based on
the Characters
Created by
CHARLES
ADDAMS

RANDOM HOUSE

WORLDS

NEW YORK

FILED

MGM

Published in the United States by RANDOM HOUSE WORLDS,
an imprint of Random House, a division of Penguin Random
House LLC, New York.

RANDOM HOUSE is a registered trademark, and RANDOM HOUSE WORLDS
and colophon are trademarks of Penguin Random House LLC.

Hardcover ISBN 978-0-593-79788-4
Ebook ISBN 978-0-593-79789-1

Printed in Canada on acid-free paper

STOCK IMAGE CREDITS: **blood splatter**—Yuliia Konakhovska/
Shutterstock; **filed stamp**—Acerebel/Getty; **hardcover texture**—
belterz/Getty; **label tape**—Jitalia17/Getty; **paper backgrounds**—
claudiodivizia/Getty, tomograf/Getty, donatas1205/Shutterstock,
Krasovski Dmitri/Shutterstock, kosmofish/Shutterstock; **paper
clip**—kolotuschenko/Getty; **photo frames**—subjug/Getty, Tolga
TEZCAN/Getty; **stamps**—IntergalacticDesignStudio/Getty;
tape—loops7/Getty, Kwangmoozaa/Getty

EDITOR: Sarah Malarkey
MANAGING EDITORS: Pam Alders and Susan Seeman
PRODUCTION EDITOR: Loren Noveck
EDITORIAL ASSISTANT: Gabriella Muñoz
DESIGNER: Laura Palese
ART DIRECTOR: Jenny Davis
PRODUCTION MANAGER: Sarah Feightner
FOOD STYLIST: Samantha Seneviratne
PROP STYLIST: Veronica Olson
PHOTOGRAPHER: Julia Gartland
PHOTO RETOUCHER: Ché Graham
COPYEDITOR: Jude Grant
PROOFREADERS: Kate Bolen, Maureen Clark,
and Marinda Valenti
INDEXER: Gina Guilinger

randomhousebooks.com

9 7 5 3   2 4 6 8

First Edition

I know I'm stubborn, single-minded, and obsessive. But those are all traits of great writers . . . and serial killers.

—WEDNESDAY ADDAMS,
Nevermore Academy student

Contents

"NEVERMORE IS LIKE NO OTHER BOARDING SCHOOL. IT'S A MAGICAL PLACE." —Gomez Addams

NEVERMORE ACADEMY

MEMORANDUM

<u>FROM:</u> The Nevermore Academy Faculty
<u>RE:</u> The Official Wednesday Cookbook

Greetings! And welcome to Nevermore Academy!

Outreach Day is here once again! This time of year, we at Nevermore Academy like to pull back the ivy and allow a sneak peek into our otherworldly operations in an effort to foster peace and harmony between Outcasts and the rest of the world. In the past, we've sent students out into your local community to volunteer their services and showcase their talents. But this year we hoped to do things a little differently (as well as sidestep some unfortunate . . . incidents . . . that may or may not have been incited by a certain now-deceased Nevermore Academy educator).

Our idea was simple. Instead of having our pupils join you in your community, we wanted to invite you to join them here at Nevermore Academy—to grant you the privilege of taking a terrifying tour behind the vaunted iron gates and see Nevermore Academy firsthand, in all its gloomy glory.

But then we talked to our board.

In the end, the powers that be decided that for the safety of all normies involved (as well as the safekeeping of some school secrets), it might be wiser to open our doors to you metaphorically instead. Which brings us to this book—an official Nevermore Academy cookbook, showcasing a taste of everything we offer at our illustrious institution.

We hope you understand.

Up until now, these recipes were kept hidden from the rest of the world in our special Nevermore Academy secret library, guarded by our illustrious alumnus Edgar Allan Poe. But now, in a gesture of goodwill, we are releasing them into the world so you and your family can re-create the macabre meals we love in the comfort of your own oh-so-normal kitchen.

A little background about our school for those of you unfamiliar: Founded in 1791 by Nathaniel Faulkner, an explorer who traveled the world cataloging Outcasts, Nevermore Academy has grown into a thriving institution and safe haven for those deemed "other." For more than two hundred years we've been nurturing and educating Outcasts, freaks, and monsters. And today we offer a rigorous academic experience, as well as world-class extracurriculars (archery, fencing, Séance Society, even beekeeping). And, most important, we help our students grow into their full potential, no matter how peculiar they might be. Whether they identify as a werewolf, vampire, siren, gorgon, shapeshifter, or psychic, our academy is a place they can all call home.

Let's be clear. This is no ordinary cookbook. Since our student body hails from all over the world (and underworld), each student comes to Nevermore Academy with their own unique tastes and dietary requirements. Which means it can be a challenge for our chefs to provide a menu varied enough to keep every student, regardless of background, feeling full, fabulous, and nonferal. Thankfully our award-winning cafeteria staff is up for the challenge, working day and night to create exceptional recipes for every appetite.

Our chefs know that vampires prefer their meals to be as bloody as possible, and werewolves mostly munch on meat. Scales are often pescatarians, preferring their food to have once swum in the sea, while gorgons tend to favor food that's hard as a rock. And then there are the particularly picky cases, like Wednesday Addams, a legacy student who came to Nevermore Academy this past semester and who insists on eating only foods as dark as her soul.

The cumulation of centuries of food research by our kitchen staff, the Nevermore Academy cookbook contains sixty recipes from all corners of the academy, ranging from bloodcurdling breakfasts, Thing's finger foods, and midday macabre meals to dinners of dark despair. We even offer up some devilish desserts and sinister sips, perfect for your next Rave'N Ball (see page 206).

In addition to our regular cafeteria fare, we invited our student body and illustrious alumni to submit their own recipes, described in their own words. Some took the assignment more seriously—and competitively—than others. Notable alumni Morticia and Gomez Addams have contributed some dishes inspired by Gomez's homeland, all with an Addams Family twist.

We have also included some legacy recipes from our Nevermore Academy vaults. (Who would have guessed that our peculiar poet laureate Edgar Allan made such a mean Poe'tato?) And no Nevermore Academy cookbook could be complete without some torturous tweaks to a few of your own classic Jericho dishes and Weathervane drinks, to help you replace yet another dull Thanksgiving with a frightful and delightful Freaksgiving Feast (see page 210). You're welcome.

We should warn you, our editors did ask us to alter a few key ingredients in some of these dark delights. For example, we regret to inform you that Uncle Fester's Scout's Honor Cookies (page 158) no longer contain any actual scouts. We also apologize that all the recipes in this book are now 100 percent nontoxic (so you can take that deadly nightshade off your shopping list). To be more inclusive of all eating habits, you'll find some suggested substitutions for those with dietary restrictions on foods that contain gluten, dairy, and human blood or require a virgin sacrifice.

So whether you're a normie looking to paint it black at your next scary soirée or are just hoping to soothe your ravenous ravens after school gets out, we hope you will enjoy this unprecedented peek into our woefully weird world and begin to realize that, at the end of the day, we are more alike than different. And that by working together we can start forming a bond between Outcasts and normies that will hopefully last . . . evermore.

Cliques and Their Cuisines:
A CHEAT SHEET

If we could impart one word of advice? Never be alone with a vamp gone vegan in a dark alley. Trust us, it does not end well.

It can be a challenge for a chef to prepare enough variety of dishes for our many Nevermore Academy cliques. Each of our students grew up with a different family menu, whether it be vampire, werewolf, siren, gorgon, shapeshifter, or psychic. But while not everyone in a clique eats like a walking, talking cliché (werewolf Enid Sinclair doesn't eat much meat for a Fur, and many vampires do not live by blood alone), we can offer some generic guidelines to go by in a pinch.

FANGS

Vampires prefer blood. But, interestingly enough, it doesn't have to come straight from the source, despite popular belief. This quirk is something we encourage, since at Nevermore Academy we've had a strict "no drinking from other students" policy in place since 1853. Instead, we import blood to create our fangfully fresh meals, desserts, and drinks sure to please every blood type.

FURS

Werewolves are usually ravenously hungry and they love meat. If given a choice, they'll pick red meat, but they'll also eat poultry, fish, pork, a sweet feral kitten—pretty much anything that once had a heartbeat. They don't always, however, want to wait patiently while we prepare their dinners, especially on nights with a full moon. Lately we've had to start locking our cafeteria freezers after dark to prevent our supplies from being wolfed down at midnight.

SCALES

Our siren friends hail from the sea and most grew up on a diet of seafood. When it comes to dinners, they prefer surf over turf, whether it be fish or shellfish or seaweed. They also tend to have sophisticated and expensive tastes—they will pick caviar over calamari every time—making them the most expensive clique to feed. In addition, they prefer their meals properly plated, so the dishes look as glamorous as they do.

STONERS

It's a well-known fact that Stoners like to snack. Instead of sitting down and eating full meals, gorgons would prefer to munch all day long and into the night. While they aren't as picky as the other cliques, they do enjoy solid food. And don't forget to keep live mice on hand at all times—their tresses get hungry!

—Nevermore Academy Head Chef

1

BLOODCURDLING
BREAKFASTS

We at Nevermore Academy believe that breakfast is the most important meal of the day, even though some of our student body prefers to stay dreaming till dusk. But, trust us, once our Outcasts do wake up from their good nightmares, they're usually ravenous and ready to head straight to the cafeteria to grab some bloodcurdling breakfast bites.

To be clear, we aren't talking about boring bacon and eggs with a side of hash browns here. The students at Nevermore Academy have very discriminating tastes, often stemming from their heritage and upbringing. In fact, there's nothing they'd abhor more than a breakfast that's basic. So we've taken it upon ourselves to survey our students to learn their preferences and then design our menus accordingly. For example, we've learned that Fangs will eat oatmeal, as long as it's topped with blood and bones (for which you can easily substitute cranberries and walnuts). Furs, on the other hand, tend to have a pack mentality and prefer their first meal of the day to be meaty. Scales, especially our sultry sirens, are extremely fond of any breakfast dish containing lox smoked straight from the sea. And the Stoners in our school will eat just about anything when they get the munchies at midnight.

Then there are our special students who march to the beat of their own drum. While one might assume roommates Wednesday Addams and Enid Sinclair would have nothing in common, it turns out they both unapologetically love waffles. And while their waffle preferences are drastically different in appearance (black as night or smothered in sprinkles), both can be created from the same batter and then . . . personalized at will. A nice shortcut for any of you who might have similar polar-opposite family members.

In addition to student favorites, we also have a few breakfast bites from our esteemed alumni Morticia and Gomez Addams. Both egg-cellent recipes, Morticia's Magnetic Migas (page 34) and Gomez's Drowned Eggs (page 37), have been modified for maximum morbidity. We've included a mail-in entry from their butler, Lurch. Evidently their son, Pugsley, insisted Lurch submit his personal recipe for a favorite breakfast treat: Pugsley's Pan de Muerto (page 38), otherwise known as Bread of the Dead. It's to die for!

We end the section with our own twist on a Weathervane Cafe & Bakery fall favorite—a quick apple bread that can be made by adding pistachio butter to give it that alluring sickly green color we all strive for in our foods. Our chefs playfully dubbed it (Poison) Apple Bread (page 43).

The next time you wake up, leave the boring breakfasts to the birds and whip up one of our Nevermore Academy specialties in your home kitchen. Whether you prefer your foods savory like a siren, as spicy as Morticia, or as sweet as Pugsley, you're sure to find a creepy concoction perfect for your morning meal.

Note: These breakfast foods pair well with the coffee drinks you'll find in part 6.

Woeful Waffles

YIELD **4** TO **6** WAFFLES,   TIME **20** MINUTES

DEPENDING ON SIZE OF WAFFLE IRON

It's probably no surprise that breakfast isn't really my thing. But when I am forced to get up and face the cruel light of morning, I want the experience to be as bleak as possible. These waffles are as black as the blissful night ripped away by the rising dawn and are the perfect reminder that the day will always fall and night will rise again. You can top them with the mournful memories of your lingering nightmares or, if you prefer something slightly less bitter, dark chocolate syrup, chocolate chips, and blackberries. Bonus: A waffle iron makes a great torture device, if you ever have to interrogate a classmate.

FILE UNDER
Wednesday

QUANTITY	INGREDIENT
1½ cups	buttermilk
5 tablespoons	unsalted butter, melted and slightly cooled
1	large egg
2 teaspoons	vanilla paste or extract
¼ cup	lightly packed light brown sugar
1½ cups	cake flour
1½ teaspoons	activated charcoal
1 teaspoon	baking powder
¾ teaspoon	baking soda
½ teaspoon	kosher salt
	Nonstick cooking spray
	Dark chocolate chips, to garnish
	Dark chocolate syrup, to garnish
	Blackberries, to serve

DIRECTIONS

1 Beat together the buttermilk, butter, egg, vanilla, and brown sugar in a large bowl until smooth. Whisk together the flour, charcoal, baking powder, baking soda, and salt in a small bowl.

2 Tip the flour mixture into the egg mixture and beat until just combined—it's okay if there are a few lumps.

3 Spray the waffle iron with cooking spray. Heat the waffle iron to medium heat, or according to the manufacturer's instructions. Cook the waffles according to the manufacturer's instructions. When the waffle iron stops steaming, that's a good sign your waffles are done—this typically takes 2 to 4 minutes, depending on the size of your waffle iron. Top the waffles with chocolate chips and a drizzle of chocolate syrup. Serve with fresh blackberries.

Whimsical Waffles

✦◇✦

YIELD 4 TO 6 WAFFLES,	TIME 20 MINUTES

DEPENDING ON SIZE OF WAFFLE IRON

FILE UNDER

Enid

While my mother says I'm supposed to eat meat for breakfast, sometimes I wake up just howling for something sweeter. So when I discovered Wednesday had brought an actual waffle iron to our dorm? I was over-the-full-moon excited! Not to mention confused. I mean, waffles? Wednesday? Of course, hers are a complete atrocity, but I discovered I can take the exact same batter—before she dyes it black—and make these super-cute creations all my own. My secret? Tons of whipped cream and brightly colored sprinkles. Also, when Wednesday caught sight of my waffles and realized they were from *her* batter? She was literally speechless with horror. Which, let's just say, made them taste all the yummier.

QUANTITY	INGREDIENT
1½ cups	buttermilk
5 tablespoons	unsalted butter, melted and slightly cooled
1	large egg
2 teaspoons	vanilla paste or extract
¼ cup	lightly packed light brown sugar
1½ cups	cake flour
2 tablespoons	rainbow sprinkles
1 teaspoon	baking powder
¾ teaspoon	baking soda
½ teaspoon	kosher salt
	Nonstick cooking spray
	Whipped cream, to garnish
	Rainbow sprinkles, to garnish
	Raspberries, to serve

DIRECTIONS

1 Beat together the buttermilk, butter, egg, vanilla, and brown sugar in a large bowl until smooth. Whisk together the flour, sprinkles, baking powder, baking soda, and salt in a small bowl.

2 Tip the flour mixture into the egg mixture and beat until just combined—it's okay if there are a few lumps.

3 Spray the waffle iron with cooking spray. Heat the waffle iron to medium heat, or according to the manufacturer's instructions. Cook the waffles according to the manufacturer's instructions. When the waffle iron stops steaming, that's a good sign your waffles are done—this typically takes 2 to 4 minutes, depending on the size of your waffle iron. Top the waffles with whipped cream and a scattering of rainbow sprinkles. Serve with fresh raspberries.

Blood & Bones Overnight Oats

YIELD **SERVES 2** | TIME **15 MINUTES PLUS OVERNIGHT REST**

A lot of people consider breakfast a morning food. But what if you are nocturnal? Even creatures of the night get hungry when they crawl out of their crypts. And on days when there's no handy blood donor in sight, this breakfast can be an amazing alternative to sink your fangs into. Unlike traditional oatmeal, these oats can be made without a microwave or a stove—which makes them a great dorm room alternative. Simply soak the oats overnight and by morning you'll have a soft mush ready to be topped by your favorite morbid mix-ins. We suggest blood and bones, but cranberries, dried cherries, and nuts will give off the same bloodstained vibe.

FILE UNDER

Fangs

QUANTITY	INGREDIENT
1 cup	rolled oats (not instant or quick-cooking)
2 cups	whole milk or plant-based milk, such as almond or oat
¼ cup	dried cranberries
¼ cup	coarsely chopped dried cherries
¼ cup	coarsely chopped pecans
3 tablespoons	pure maple syrup
½ teaspoon	kosher salt
½ teaspoon	ground cinnamon
2 tablespoons	red jam, such as strawberry, cherry, or raspberry
	Slivered almonds, to garnish

DIRECTIONS

1 If you have access to a stove, you can start by toasting the oats in a medium stainless-steel skillet over medium-high heat, tossing and stirring occasionally, until lightly browned, 5 to 8 minutes. Let cool slightly. Place the oats (whether toasted or not) in a large sealable container.

2 Stir in the milk, cranberries, cherries, pecans, maple syrup, salt, and cinnamon. Cover the container, and refrigerate overnight.

3 Divide the overnight oats between two bowls. Top each bowl with 1 tablespoon red jam of your choice. Scatter slivered almonds over the top of each bowl and serve.

Real Wolves Eat Quiche

✦○✦

YIELD **1** DEEP-DISH 9-INCH QUICHE │ TIME **75** MINUTES PREP,
45 TO **50** MINUTES BAKING

Every alpha knows that their pack will wake up ravenous after a night of rock-
ing out under a full moon. But never fear: This rich and eggy recipe will soothe
even the most savage of beasts. Packed with protein, it'll get them through the
school day and allow them to wolf out with their friends again that night. And
while it can be made entirely vegetarian, we suggest adding ham, bacon, and
sausage to make it extra Fur-friendly. Trust us, you won't be a lone wolf for
long after whipping up this meaty masterpiece.

QUANTITY	INGREDIENT
	CRUST
1½ cups	all-purpose flour, plus more for the work surface
1 teaspoon	sugar
¾ teaspoon	kosher salt
8 tablespoons (1 stick)	unsalted butter, cut into ½-inch cubes
3 tablespoons	cold water
	FILLING
4 ounces	ground breakfast sausage
4 ounces	pancetta or thick-cut bacon, diced
3 slices	deli ham, torn into bite-size pieces
4	large eggs
1 cup	heavy cream
½ teaspoon	kosher salt
¼ teaspoon	freshly ground black pepper
⅔ cup	shredded Cheddar cheese
⅔ cup	shredded Gouda cheese

DIRECTIONS

1 *Make the crust:* Place the flour, sugar, salt, and butter in the bowl of a food processor. Pulse to combine, until the mixture resembles wet sand, about 2 minutes.

2 Transfer the contents of the food processor to a large bowl. Add the cold water and stir until a shaggy dough forms. Knead the dough with your hands until fairly smooth, about 2 minutes. Shape the dough into a disc, wrap with plastic wrap, and refrigerate for 1 hour.

3 *While the dough chills, make the filling:* Cook the sausage and pancetta in a skillet over medium-high heat, breaking apart the sausage with a wooden spoon. Continue cooking until the sausage and pancetta are crispy and cooked through, 10 to 15 minutes. Drain off and discard any excess fat. Add the deli ham, and set aside the mixture to cool slightly.

4 Beat together the eggs, heavy cream, salt, and pepper in a small bowl until smooth. Toss together both cheeses in a separate small bowl. Set aside.

5 Place an oven rack in the lower third position of the oven. Heat the oven to 375°F.

6 Turn out the chilled dough onto a lightly floured surface and roll out to a thickness of ¼ inch. Carefully transfer the dough to a pie plate. Trim the dough, leaving a ½-inch overhang, then crimp the edges.

THE RECIPE CONTINUES

QUANTITY	INGREDIENT	DIRECTIONS (CONT.)

7 Scatter half the cheese on the bottom of the piecrust, then all the sausage-pancetta mixture. Slowly pour the egg mixture into the pie shell, allowing it to fill in all the empty spaces. Top with the remaining cheese.

8 Transfer the pie plate to a half-sheet pan. Bake for 45 to 50 minutes, until the crust is golden brown and the filling is puffed and just barely set—it's okay if the very center wobbles slightly. Let cool for 10 to 15 minutes before slicing and serving. Wrap any leftover quiche tightly with foil and store in the fridge for up to 3 days.

COOK'S NOTE: Serve leftovers cold or at room temperature. If you prefer to have it warm, heat in the microwave for 1 minute or in the oven at 325°F for 10 minutes.

Siren Salmon & Seaweed Toast

YIELD **SERVES 4**   TIME **10** MINUTES

Haters gonna hate, but every siren knows they're just jealous that we've come up with the most *fintastically* healthy and hearty way to start off a siren's day swimmingly. There's absolutely nothing basic about this avocado toast topped with arugula "seaweed" (for you normies) and smoked salmon. Add a poached egg and a sprinkle of goat cheese if you're feeling a surf-and-turf vibe. And don't apologize for your good taste. Remember, you can't be a queen bee without a little bougie breakfast.

QUANTITY	INGREDIENT
2	ripe avocados, halved and pitted
	Zest and juice of 1 lemon
	Pinch of kosher salt, plus more as needed
4 slices	crusty sourdough bread
½ cup	microgreens, such as arugula
2 ounces	smoked salmon
8	multicolored grape tomatoes, sliced into ¼-inch-thick coins
	Freshly ground black pepper

DIRECTIONS

1 Scoop the avocado into a medium bowl. Add lemon juice and a good pinch of salt. Mash until somewhat smooth, with some small chunks of avocado remaining. Season to taste with additional salt if needed.

2 Toast the bread until deep golden brown. Let cool slightly, then distribute the smashed avocado evenly onto each slice. Spread the avocado to the edges of each slice with the back of a spoon.

3 Scatter the microgreens evenly over each slice of toast. Break apart or tear the smoked salmon into 16 to 20 irregular bite-size pieces. Nestle 4 or 5 pieces of salmon into the microgreens on each slice of toast.

4 Tuck the tomato slices between the pieces of salmon on each slice of toast—alternate the colors of tomato for an extra-pretty presentation. Season with pepper and reserved lemon zest and serve.

Fire & Brimscones

+◇+

YIELD	12 SCONES	TIME	15 MINUTES PREP,
			20 TO 25 MINUTES BAKING

Let's face it, mornings can be really rocky for Stoners. But these fiery scones are guaranteed to rock your taste buds. They are as dry as a stone on the outside, with a hot-as-hell surprise when you take that first bite (thanks to some secret Calabrian chiles mixed into the dough). It's sure to make your snakes stand on end! (Just make sure you respect your fellow students and keep those snakes covered in the cafeteria, please. Turning into stone will no longer be considered an approved excuse for tardiness.)

FILE UNDER
Stoners

QUANTITY	INGREDIENT
3 cups	all-purpose flour
1½ teaspoons	kosher salt
1 tablespoon	baking powder
8 tablespoons (1 stick)	unsalted butter, cut into ½-inch cubes
1 tablespoon	chopped Calabrian chiles (see Cook's Note)
4 ounces	Manchego cheese, shredded (1 cup)
2 ounces	prosciutto, torn into bite-size pieces
1¼ cups	heavy cream

DIRECTIONS

1 Heat the oven to 350°F. Line a half-sheet pan with parchment paper and set aside.

2 Place the flour, salt, baking powder, butter, and chiles in the bowl of a food processor. Pulse until the mixture resembles wet sand, with some pea-size bits of butter remaining.

3 Tip the contents of the food processor into a large bowl. Add about three-quarters of the cheese, reserving the rest. Add the prosciutto, then toss to combine. Stir in the heavy cream. Mix until incorporated and the dough is relatively smooth, kneading with your hands if necessary.

4 Divide the dough into 12 equal portions using an ice cream scoop. Roll each piece of dough into a rough ball and arrange on the prepared sheet pan. Gently flatten the dough balls with the palm of your hand, then sprinkle with the reserved cheese. Bake until golden brown, 20 to 25 minutes. Transfer to a wire rack to let cool. Serve warm or at room temperature.

COOK'S NOTE: Calabrian chiles are bright, flavorful, and spicy, and are usually found jarred in oil. If you prefer a less spicy scone, reduce by half or omit altogether.

Morticia's Magnetic Migas

YIELD SERVES 4 TO 6	TIME 20 MINUTES

Nevermore Academy is the place Gomez and I first fell in love and began a courtship that has lasted a lifetime. Back then, we sometimes skipped out on sleeping to spend the entire night roaming the local graveyards. Making out on top of tombstones until dawn can leave one ravenous for something beyond an undying love. So on those mornings, I would whip up one of mi amor's favorite dishes—a Mexican scramble of eggs, tortilla strips, and cheese. Add chorizo sausage (or its plant-based cousin, "soyrizo") for a breakfast that's as sultry as any cemetery.

QUANTITY	INGREDIENT
10	large eggs
½ teaspoon	kosher salt
1 tablespoon	neutral oil, such as canola or grapeseed
8 ounces	chorizo or soyrizo
2 cups	crumbled tortilla chips
½ cup	shredded Oaxaca or Monterey Jack cheese
	Soul-Sucking Salsa (page 48) or other hot sauce, to serve (optional)

DIRECTIONS

1 Whisk together the eggs and salt in a large bowl until homogenous and slightly frothy. Set aside.

2 Heat the oil in a 10-inch skillet over medium-high heat. Add the chorizo or soyrizo and cook, stirring frequently, until crispy, about 10 minutes. Add the crumbled tortilla chips and toss to coat.

3 Reduce the heat to medium, then add the eggs. Cook, stirring constantly, until the eggs are just barely set and still moist, 5 to 7 minutes. Sprinkle the shredded cheese over the top, then cover the skillet for 1 to 2 minutes, until the cheese has melted and the eggs are set. Serve with Soul-Sucking Salsa on the side, if desired.

> "Seeing you in handcuffs, accused of murder? I've never loved you more!"
>
> —MORTICIA ADDAMS

Gomez's Drowned Eggs

| YIELD | SERVES 4 | TIME | 30 TO 35 MINUTES |

I think everyone in my family knows that I'd rather drown in a deep, dark, endless ocean than be without my cara bella for even a single night. And thanks to my daughter Wednesday's psychic investigation into Garrett Gates's murder, I've once again been acquitted, allowing me to return to Morticia's loving arms. Which means these days the only thing that needs drowning are these eggs poached in a pan of salsa—while I'm making Tish's favorite breakfast dish. They're simple, satisfying, and as spicy as our love affair.

QUANTITY	INGREDIENT
2 tablespoons	olive oil
1	medium yellow onion, diced
1	jalapeño or serrano chile, stem and seeds removed, finely chopped
2	garlic cloves, finely chopped
1 pound	tomatillos, husked and quartered
2 cups	low-sodium chicken stock
½ teaspoon	ground cumin
1 teaspoon	kosher salt, plus more as needed
½ teaspoon	freshly ground black pepper
8	large eggs
	Crumbled Cotija cheese, to serve
	Warm tortillas, to serve

DIRECTIONS

1 Heat the olive oil in a high-walled, 10-inch stainless-steel sauté pan over medium-high heat until shimmering (the oil will seem to move on its own). Add the onion and cook, stirring occasionally, until softened and just beginning to turn brown on the edges, 10 to 12 minutes.

2 Add the chile and garlic and cook, stirring constantly, until fragrant, about 1 minute. Add the tomatillos. Cook, stirring occasionally, until the tomatillos start to break down and release their juices, 10 to 15 minutes. If you notice other ingredients start to darken too quickly, reduce the heat to medium.

3 Add the chicken stock to the pan, then remove from the heat. Transfer the mixture to a blender or the bowl of a food processor. Add the cumin, salt, and pepper. Pulse until fairly smooth, 2 to 3 minutes. Season to taste with additional salt, if needed.

4 Return the salsa to the skillet and bring to a boil over medium-high heat. Reduce to a simmer, then add the eggs, one at a time, to the salsa, leaving ½ inch or so of space between each one. Seven should fit comfortably around the outer perimeter with enough space for one more in the center.

5 Cover the skillet and let simmer until the egg whites are set but the yolks are still soft, 3 to 5 minutes. Divide the eggs and salsa among four bowls and serve with the cheese and tortillas alongside.

Pugsley's Pan de Muerto

+○

YIELD **1** LOAF   TIME **6** HOURS PREP, **12** TO **36** HOURS CHILLING, **20** TO **25** MINUTES BAKING

It's been hard not having my sister at home these days. There's no one left to attempt first-degree murder against those who make fun of me at school. But there are some silver linings to a world without Wednesday. Like I no longer have to share my favorite breakfast treat, Pan de Muerto (Bread of the Dead), with anyone else. Lurch makes it best, shaping the sweet bread into this round dish with bones jutting out from all directions and a skull on top (not a real one, sadly; he says those would be too hard to chew). Also, he says if you eat it on Día de Muertos (Day of the Dead), it will feed your dead relatives' spirits.

QUANTITY	INGREDIENT	DIRECTIONS
½ cup	lukewarm whole milk	**1** Whisk together the milk and yeast in a small bowl. Set aside for 5 to 10 minutes, until you notice a few bubbles on the surface.
1½ teaspoons	active dry yeast	
1	large egg	**2** In the bowl of a stand mixer, use a fork to beat together the egg, sugar, orange zest, vanilla, orange blossom water, aniseed, salt, cinnamon, and allspice until combined. Attach the dough hook to the mixer. Add the flour and the milk mixture and mix on low speed until a shaggy dough forms, 3 to 5 minutes.
3 tablespoons	sugar, plus more for sprinkling	
	Zest of 1 orange	
1 teaspoon	vanilla extract	
½ teaspoon	orange blossom water	**3** Increase the speed of the mixer to medium and knead until smooth, 10 to 15 minutes. Add 2 tablespoons of the softened butter and continue mixing until the butter is completely incorporated, 2 to 3 minutes. Repeat with the remaining 4 tablespoons softened butter.
1 teaspoon	whole aniseed	
¾ teaspoon	kosher salt	
½ teaspoon	ground cinnamon	
¼ teaspoon	ground allspice	
2 cups	bread flour	**4** Increase the mixer speed to medium-high and knead for 15 to 20 minutes, until the dough is smooth and elastic and passes the windowpane test. (This is when you take a small piece of dough and stretch it between your fingers. You should be able to stretch it thin enough to see through it without the dough tearing. If the dough tears easily, continue kneading for 5 minutes, then repeat the test.)
6 tablespoons (¾ stick)	unsalted butter, softened	
	Nonstick cooking spray	
1 tablespoon	unsalted butter, melted	**5** Spray the inside of a large bowl with cooking spray. Transfer the dough to the bowl and cover with plastic wrap. Let the dough sit in a warm, draft-free spot in your kitchen until doubled in volume, 60 to 90 minutes.

6 Deflate the dough by gently pressing down on it with a closed fist. Starting at the right side of the bowl, lift the dough and fold it up on itself. Rotate the bowl 90 degrees and repeat. Do this two more times. Cover the bowl with the same sheet of plastic wrap, and transfer the bowl to the fridge. Let the dough rest for 12 to 36 hours (the longer you leave the dough in the fridge, the more flavorful it will become).

7 Line a half-sheet pan with parchment paper and set aside. Remove the dough from the fridge and let it sit in the covered bowl for 2 hours to come to room temperature. It should get puffy but not necessarily double in volume.

8 Turn out the dough onto a clean work surface. Using a bench scraper or sharp knife, cut off about one-quarter of the dough. Set this aside.

9 Shape the larger piece of dough into a smooth ball. Place the dough on the work surface and gently cup the sides of the dough with your hands. Spin the dough clockwise with your cupped hands. The friction of the dough spinning on the work surface will slowly pull the top of the dough taut—stop once the top of the dough is smooth and domed. Carefully transfer the dough to the prepared sheet pan, then press down on it slightly to flatten with the palm of your hand—the dough should be roughly 6 inches in diameter.

10 Shape the skull and crossbones from the smaller piece of dough. Cut off one-quarter of the smaller piece of dough and shape it into a ball. This time, cup your hand over the top of the dough with your fingers on the work surface. Slowly rotate your hand over the dough to shape it into a ball. Set this aside. Cut the remaining larger piece of dough into 2 equal pieces and roll them into two 6-inch logs.

11 Pinch the center of each log to flatten. Transfer both pieces to the top of the large dough ball, overlapping the flattened centers to form a cross. Pinch both logs from where they cross out toward both ends to create thinner sections of "bone." Finally, place the small dough ball in the center of the crossbones, pressing down gently. Spray a sheet of plastic wrap with cooking spray and drape it over the loaf. Let rise until doubled in volume, 60 to 90 minutes.

12 Toward the end of the rising time, heat the oven to 350°F. Once the dough has doubled in volume, remove the plastic wrap and bake until golden brown, 20 to 25 minutes. Let the bread cool for 5 minutes, then transfer to a wire rack set in a half-sheet pan. Brush half of the top of the loaf with half of the melted butter, then immediately sprinkle generously with sugar before the butter has a chance to dry. Repeat the process to coat the other half of the loaf. Let cool to room temperature before slicing and serving. Bread may be stored tightly wrapped in plastic wrap at room temperature for up to 3 days.

COOK'S NOTE: Pan de Muerto is best (and commonly!) served with a steamy mug of Mexican hot chocolate, also called champurrado; see Mija's Mud (page 188).

What Is Día de Muertos?

Día de Muertos, known as Day of the Dead in English, is a holiday widely celebrated in Mexican cultures that takes place the two days after Halloween. While these days are reserved for remembrance of friends and family who have died, it's not a solemn occasion but rather a joyous celebration of their lives. Families create home altars for their deceased family members, exchange sugar skulls, and bake their favorite foods in their loved ones' honor while sharing stories about their lives. A favorite treat is Pan de Muerto (Bread of the Dead), which is topped with dough shaped into skulls and crossbones. The holiday is observed in Mexico as well as in other countries, including Brazil, El Salvador, the Philippines, and parts of the United States.

(Poison) Apple Bread

✦◆✦◇

YIELD	1 LOAF	TIME	15 MINUTES PREP, 65 TO 75 MINUTES BAKING

We hate to admit it, but sometimes you normies get it right. Case in point, this classic breakfast bread served at the Weathervane in neighboring Jericho. Based on an old Depression-era recipe, it requires no yeast and no time to rise. We've given this bread a Nevermore Academy twist by adding pistachio butter, which imparts a sickening green hue. This apple bread is everything you could want for festive fall flair.

QUANTITY	INGREDIENT
	Nonstick cooking spray
2 cups	all-purpose flour
1 tablespoon	baking powder
1 teaspoon	ground cinnamon
¼ teaspoon	ground cloves
¼ teaspoon	ground cardamom
½ cup	pistachio butter
1 cup	apple cider
½ cup	heavy cream
½ cup	lightly packed light brown sugar
1 teaspoon	vanilla extract
½ teaspoon	pistachio extract
2 drops	bright green gel food coloring (optional)
1	green apple, peeled, cored, and diced
2 tablespoons	raw sugar
	Salted butter, softened, to serve (optional)

DIRECTIONS

1. Heat the oven to 350°F. Grease an 8½ × 4½-inch loaf pan with cooking spray.

2. Whisk together the flour, baking powder, cinnamon, cloves, and cardamom in a medium bowl. Set aside.

3. Whisk together the pistachio butter, apple cider, heavy cream, brown sugar, vanilla, pistachio extract, and, if using, the food coloring in a large bowl. Stir in the flour mixture and beat until just combined and no dry flour remains. Fold in the apple.

4. Scrape the batter into the prepared loaf pan and smooth the surface into an even layer with a rubber spatula. Sprinkle the raw sugar evenly over the top of the batter.

5. Bake until a cake tester comes out clean, with a few moist crumbs clinging to it, when inserted into the center of the bread, 65 to 75 minutes. Let cool in the pan for 5 minutes, then turn out the loaf onto a wire rack to cool completely before slicing. Serve as is or with a smear of softened salted butter.

2

THING'S
FINGER
FOODS

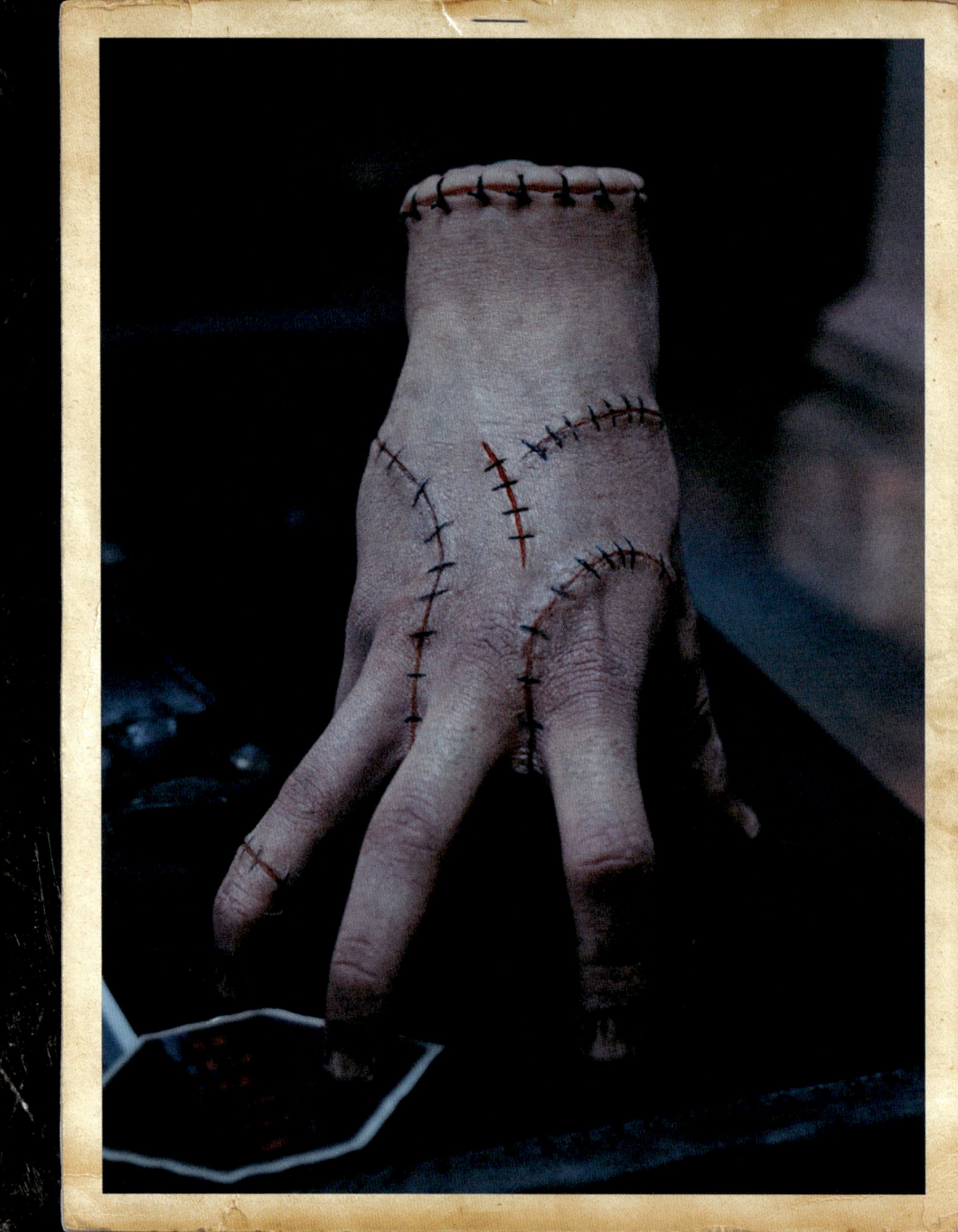

Everyone likes a good snack, even our Outcasts. While we faithfully serve three meals a day at the Nevermore Academy cafeteria, we've found that sometimes our students just need a quick and simple (and often slimy) snack to help them power through afternoon classes and keep their inner beast at bay. This is why we've introduced these fun-size finger foods—none of which, incidentally, call for any real fingers to make (something Wednesday's right-hand man, Thing, can surely appreciate).

In addition to feeding hungry students, these finger foods can double as appealing appetizers at your next dark dinner party or date night in. Or they can be made in larger batches to put out on a table at your next Rave'N Ball or post–Poe Cup party.

While you'll find more choices in this section than you can count on one hand, two of our favorite entries once again come from our most unlikely of roommates. Wednesday loves dipping tortilla chips into her homemade Soul-Sucking Salsa (page 48).

Enid, on the other hand, favors a recipe she's dubbed Pink Puppy Chow (page 53), a sweet, crunchy cereal mix made with chocolate, powdered sugar, and freeze-dried strawberry powder to give it that special Enid-approved pink vibe. It's cute, it's crunchy, and it's perfect for late-night dorm room dance parties or studying for finals.

We've also included snacks from our various cliques. The Fangs, for example, enjoy these sweet and savory Blackened Buffalo Bat Wings (page 56), which don't require any actual bats . . . or buffalo, for that matter. The Furs like to munch on meaty Full-Moon Franks (page 59), their twist on traditional pigs in a blanket. For Stoners, we offer a Mummified Brie (page 60), a soft cheese covered in pastry strips. It's hard on the outside but nice and gooey once you break through its stony shell.

Readers will find a nod to our own disturbing history with an original recipe from the evil Joseph Crackstone, who tried to burn witches and destroy all Outcasts. Thanks to Goody Addams, he ultimately failed in his quest, but his Salt & Burn the Bones (page 63) remains with us to this day. And we think you'll admit it's on fire.

So the next time you feel sucky or snacky, try whipping up one of these fun finger foods. They're hands-down delicious and will single-handedly hold you over until dinner.

Soul-Sucking Salsa & Chips

✦◦✦

| YIELD | ABOUT 2 CUPS | TIME | 45 MINUTES |

When writing my novel, playing my cello, or plotting nefarious ways to disembowel those pathetic souls who dare get in my way, sometimes I admittedly get hungry. Since most of the so-called snacks at Nevermore Academy are far too colorful for my taste or contain enough sugar to make one insufferably hyper for hours on end (see: Enid, always), I'll sometimes ask Thing to whip me up my favorite discomfort food from home. Perfect for those allergic to color, this monochromatic mash-up features white corn tortilla chips accompanied with a salsa negra as dark as my world-weary soul. It's spicy enough to murder your taste buds, and the crunch will wake the dead—or at least my roommate.

FILE UNDER *Wednesday*

QUANTITY	INGREDIENT
2	plum tomatoes, cored and halved
1	small red onion, quartered
1	serrano chile, stem removed (see Cook's Note)
1 ounce	dried guajillo chiles, stems and seeds removed
2 ounces	dried pasilla negra chiles, stems and seeds removed
¼ cup	olive oil
2 teaspoons	black garlic puree
¼ cup	black sesame seeds
2 teaspoons	ground coriander
1 teaspoon	ground cumin
¼ teaspoon	ground cloves
½ teaspoon	kosher salt
1 tablespoon	soy sauce
	Juice of 1 lime (about 2 tablespoons)
	Tortilla chips, to serve

DIRECTIONS

1 Place an oven rack directly under the broiler. Heat the oven to broil.

2 Line a quarter-sheet pan with foil. Place the tomatoes, skin side up, onion, and serrano chile on the prepared sheet pan and broil until well charred, 10 to 12 minutes. Flip the onion and serrano about halfway through to ensure even charring. Set aside to cool slightly.

3 While the vegetables cook, heat the guajillo and pasilla chiles in a medium saucepan over medium-high heat, stirring occasionally, until the chiles are toasted and pliable, 3 to 5 minutes. Cover the chiles with water, then bring to a boil. Cover the saucepan and remove from the heat. Let sit for 15 minutes to allow the chiles to rehydrate.

4 Place the charred vegetables in the bowl of a food processor. Scoop the chiles from the saucepan with a slotted spoon and transfer to the food processor. Reserve the soaking liquid.

5 Add the olive oil, black garlic puree, sesame seeds, coriander, cumin, cloves, salt, and soy sauce to the food processor, along with ½ cup of the reserved soaking liquid. Pulse until smooth, 1 to 2 minutes. If the salsa is too thick, add more of the reserved soaking liquid. Add the lime juice, then pulse to combine. Serve with tortilla chips as a snack. This salsa is also a perfect condiment to serve alongside other dishes, like Morticia's Magnetic Migas (page 34). Store leftover salsa in an airtight container in the fridge for up to 1 week.

COOK'S NOTE: This isn't a particularly hot salsa, but you can make it milder by removing the ribs and seeds from the serrano. To go even milder, substitute a stemmed, seeded jalapeño for the serrano.

LEGACY STUDENT SPOTLIGHT
Wednesday Addams

WEDNESDAY ADDAMS started her education in a public school, but her alumni parents eventually saw the wisdom of enrolling her in an institution with more like-minded peers after she attempted (and failed) to murder the swim team with live piranha and got herself expelled.

The only daughter of Morticia and Gomez Addams, Wednesday is a legacy student with a very strong pedigree. She's even distantly related to Goody Addams, who formed the original Nightshade Society to protect and fight for the Outcasts back in the 1600s.

That said, we've found Wednesday to be quite stubborn during her brief time at Nevermore Academy. She always says and does exactly what she wants, even at times when her authority figures and peers try to persuade her otherwise. We do know she qualifies as an Outcast, thanks to her psychic powers, though her supposed allergy to color has yet to be confirmed. We err on the side of caution, though. Rather than make a student break out in hives and have their flesh peel off their bones, we try to respect all dietary restrictions, even those related to color.

While Wednesday can come off as brittle and uncaring, her two best Nevermore Academy friends, Enid and Eugene, would argue that beneath that hard shell lies a good and caring friend who will do just about anything to help you out in a time of need. In fact, she once threatened to break gorgon Ajax's face if he broke Enid's heart. A sign of a true friend.

Wednesday is also a writer, an amateur detective, and a member of the Hummers. She loves rainstorms, funerals, and daydreaming of death. She would prefer that you not speak to her. Ever.

> "I actually fillet the
> bodies of my victims, then feed them
> to my menagerie of pets."
> —WEDNESDAY ADDAMS

Pink Puppy Chow

◆○◆

YIELD	ABOUT 4 CUPS	TIME	15 MINUTES PLUS COOLING TIME

FILE UNDER

Enid

Let's face it, late-night dorm room dance parties can leave you literally starving! So when the caf is closed, I like to whip up this super-sweet, super-yummy snack to keep my inner wolf at bay. Full disclosure, it kind of looks like dog food, hence the name, but trust me, this is some quality kibble. Think crunchy cereal dipped in nutty melted chocolate, then coated with powdered sugar. I mean, YUM, right? Also, my version is even better than the stuff my mom used to make, because it's pink, and pink makes everything better (well, except for Wednesday's general mood, but that's not my problem).

QUANTITY	INGREDIENT	DIRECTIONS
4 cups	crisp rice, corn, or wheat square cereal, or a combination	**1** Line a half-sheet pan with parchment paper and set aside.
1 cup	powdered sugar	**2** Place the cereal squares in a large bowl. Sift together the powdered sugar and strawberry powder in a small bowl. Set aside.
⅓ cup	freeze-dried strawberry or raspberry powder	
½ cup	bittersweet chocolate chips	**3** Place the chocolate, sunflower butter, unsalted butter, and vanilla in a medium heatproof bowl over a small saucepan of simmering water (be sure the bottom of the bowl isn't touching the water). Gently heat the chocolate mixture, stirring occasionally, until smooth. Stir in vanilla.
¼ cup	sunflower butter or any nut butter	
2 tablespoons	unsalted butter	**4** Pour the chocolate mixture over the cereal. Gently stir and toss until evenly coated. Transfer the cereal to a gallon-size plastic ziplock bag, then pour in the powdered sugar mixture. Seal the bag and shake to coat.
1 teaspoon	vanilla extract	
		5 Transfer the puppy chow to the prepared sheet pan and spread out evenly. Let cool completely. Store leftover puppy chow in an airtight container at room temperature for up to 1 week.

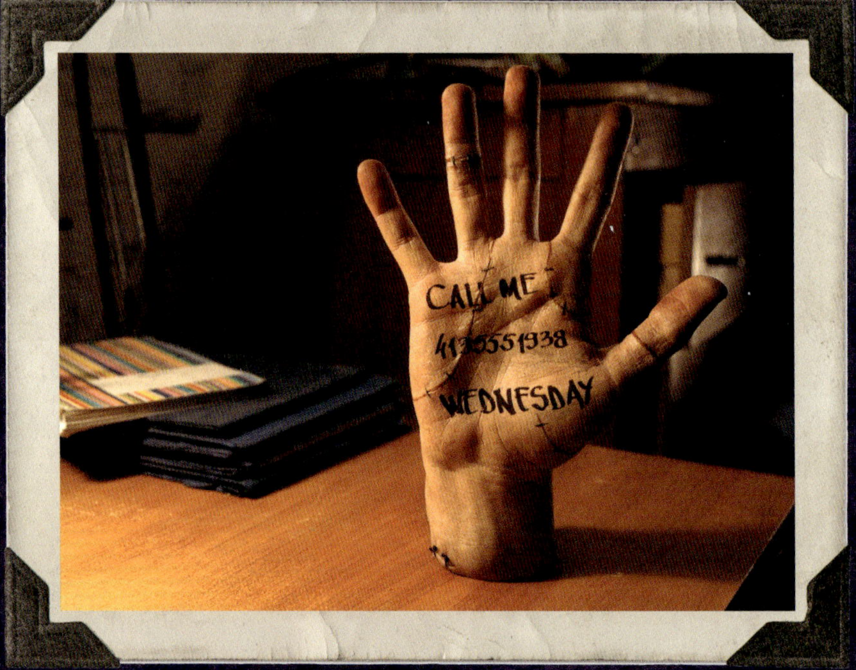
CALL ME
4135551938
WEDNESDAY

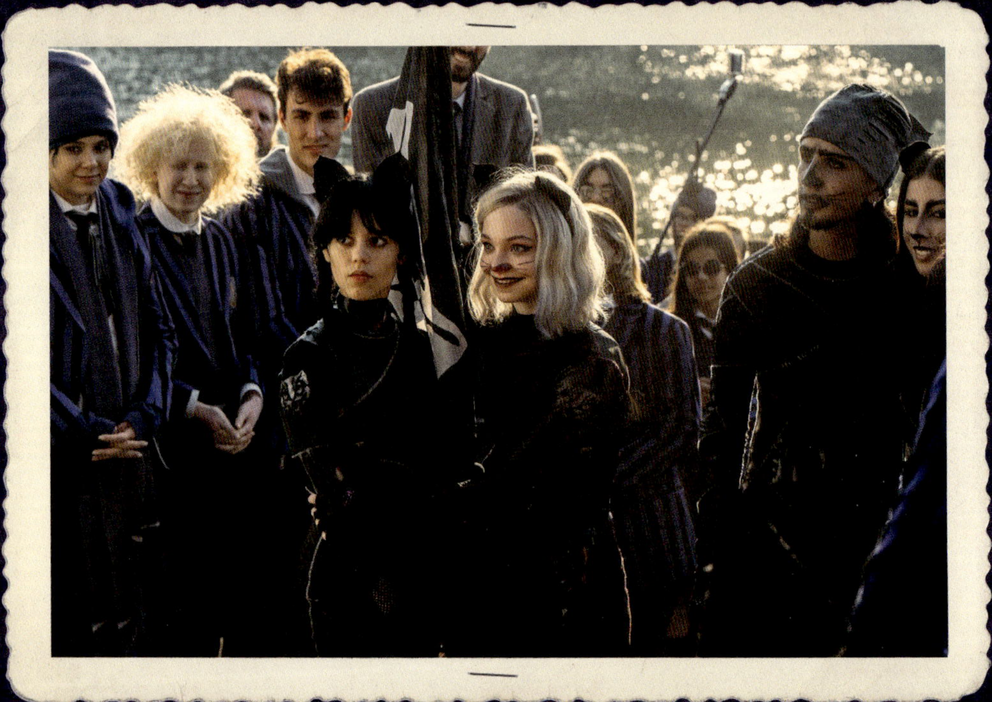

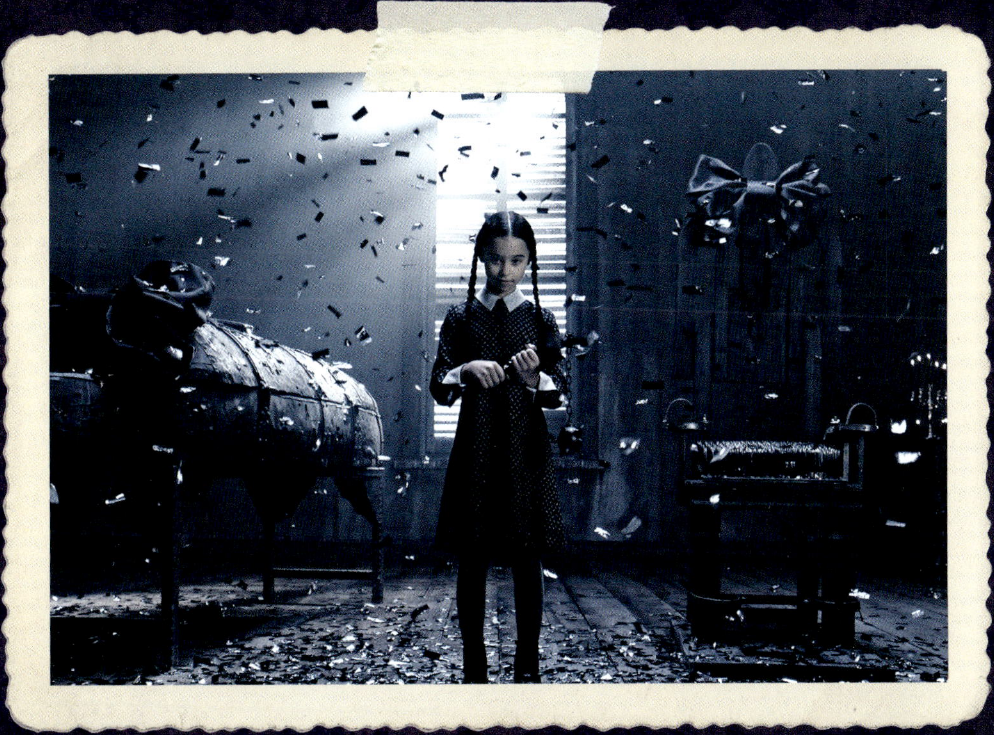

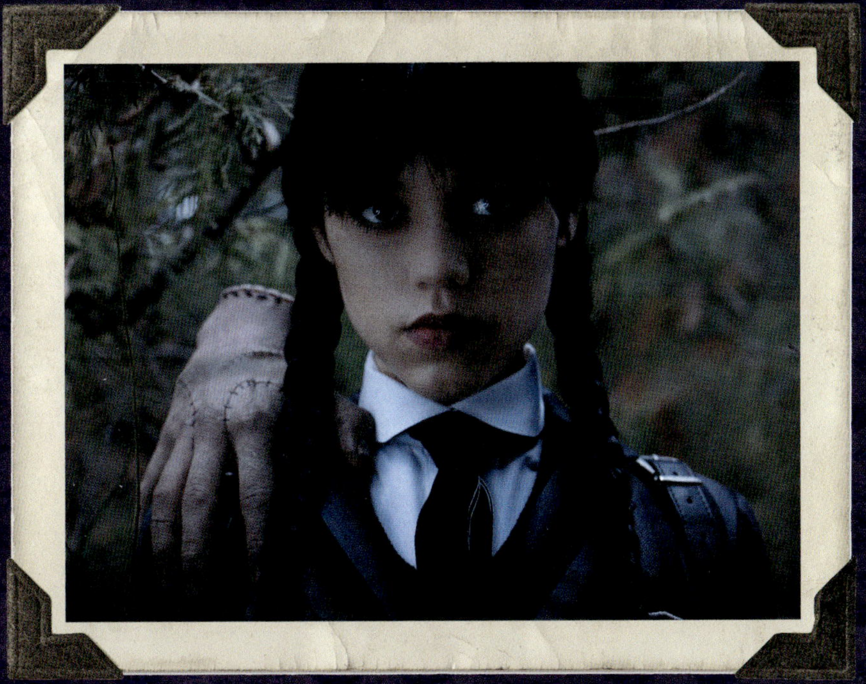

Blackened Buffalo Bat Wings

❖◦❖

YIELD   SERVES **4**

TIME **20** MINUTES PREP,
40 TO **45** MINUTES COOKING

It's a well-known fact among vampire circles that bats are the new chicken. And if you've never tasted a blackened buffalo bat wing, you clearly haven't died. However, we do understand some readers may have an aversion to eating bats (evidently rabies is a concern for your immune systems?), so we've adapted our two-thousand-year-old secret recipe to be made with chicken wings instead while keeping with the dark aesthetic of the dish. Using a glaze of maple syrup, black sesame, black vinegar, and sesame oil (and black garlic for those of you who aren't allergic!), you'll be able to create a sweet and savory snack that pairs perfectly with O-negative.

FILE UNDER

Fangs

QUANTITY	INGREDIENT
	SAUCE
⅓ cup	pure maple syrup
3 tablespoons	soy sauce
3 tablespoons	black vinegar
2 tablespoons	gochujang
1 tablespoon	black garlic puree
1 teaspoon	black sesame paste
1 tablespoon	toasted sesame oil
	WINGS
	Nonstick cooking spray
2 pounds	chicken wings, patted dry with paper towels
2 teaspoons	kosher salt
1 teaspoon	freshly ground black pepper

DIRECTIONS

1 *Make the sauce:* Whisk together the maple syrup, soy sauce, vinegar, gochujang, black garlic puree, and black sesame paste in a small saucepan. Bring to a simmer over medium heat and cook, stirring occasionally, until reduced and thickened, 10 to 15 minutes. Remove from the heat and stir in the sesame oil.

2 *Make the wings:* Heat the oven to 400°F. Place an ovenproof wire rack in a half-sheet pan. Lightly coat the rack with cooking spray. Arrange the wings on the wire rack, leaving space between each wing. Season with the salt and pepper.

3 Roast the wings until crispy and golden brown all over, 40 to 45 minutes, flipping the wings halfway through cooking to ensure even crisping. Transfer the wings to a large heatproof bowl. Drizzle with the prepared sauce. Toss to coat, and serve immediately. Leftovers can be stored in the fridge in an airtight container for up to 3 days.

Full-Moon Franks

YIELD ABOUT 2 DOZEN

TIME 15 MINUTES PREP,
20 TO 25 MINUTES COOKING

FILE UNDER

FURS

Howling at the moon can make one hungry! So when the pack's whining, you might want to whip up this quick and tasty treat to get them to heel. While Furs usually hunt for their own meat under the light of a full moon, if you're not up to wolfing out, you can always use cocktail wieners, little sausages, or even regular hot dogs, cut into quarters. Wrapped in flaky pastry and served with a side of mustard and ketchup, these franks are so doggone good, you won't be able to wolf down just one.

QUANTITY	INGREDIENT	DIRECTIONS
1 sheet	frozen puff pastry	**1** Heat the oven to 425°F. Line a half-sheet pan with parchment paper and set aside.
	All-purpose flour, for the work surface	
2 tablespoons	Dijon mustard, plus more to serve	**2** Thaw the puff pastry according to the package instructions. It should be cold but pliable. Place the pastry sheet on a lightly floured work surface. Roll out to a 12 × 14-inch rectangle, about ⅛ inch thick. Brush the mustard all over in a thin, even layer.
1 12-ounce package	cocktail franks, drained and patted dry	
1	large egg	
2 tablespoons	everything bagel seasoning	**3** Using a bench scraper or pizza cutter, cut twenty-four 1 × 2½-inch rectangles out of the dough (you will have extra dough, which you can discard or use for another purpose). Wrap each cocktail frank with a rectangle of pastry, pinching the seam together to seal. Transfer the franks to the prepared sheet pan as you go.
	Ketchup, to serve	

4 Beat the egg with 1 tablespoon water in a small bowl until smooth. Brush the top of each pig in a blanket with a thin layer of the egg mixture. Sprinkle the top with everything bagel seasoning. Bake for 20 to 25 minutes, until puffed and golden brown. Serve hot with mustard and ketchup alongside.

Mummified Brie

YIELD SERVES 6 TO 8   **TIME** 10 MINUTES PREP, 35 MINUTES COOKING

Even though Stoners might seem a little tough on the outside, once you manage to break through our shells, you'll find we can actually be quite soft and sweet, just like our favorite Stoner snack: baked Brie wrapped in flaky pastry. This particular variation, perfect for the Halloween season, uses strips of pastry wrapped around the cheese, giving it a mummified motif. Once it's cooked, cutting through the crust reveals a soft and gooey cheese, perfect to pair with stoned wheat crackers or your favorite dipper. A cheese-tastic choice for your next creepover.

QUANTITY	INGREDIENT
1 sheet	frozen puff pastry
1	large egg
	All-purpose flour, for the work surface
1	wheel of cold Brie (6 to 8 ounces)
1 tablespoon	jam, such as fig or tart cherry
	Crackers, to serve

DIRECTIONS

1 Heat the oven to 425°F. Line a half-sheet pan with parchment paper. Thaw the puff pastry according to the package instructions. It should be cold but pliable.

2 Beat the egg with 1 tablespoon water in a small bowl until smooth. Place the pastry sheet on a lightly floured work surface. Roll out to a thickness of about ⅛ inch. Brush all over with a thin layer of the egg mixture, reserving the leftover mixture for later. Cut down the middle with a bench scraper or pizza cutter. Set aside one of the pastry halves.

3 Place the cheese wheel at one end of the other puff pastry half, then spread the jam over the top of the wheel in a thin, even layer. Fold the other end of the pastry over the cheese, tucking the dough in and around it. Press down around the edges to seal the pastry, then trim a circle around it, leaving a border of about ¼ inch. Transfer the wrapped cheese to the prepared sheet pan.

4 Cut the reserved pastry half lengthwise into strips ranging from ½ inch to 1 inch wide. Drape a few strips, wet side down, over the cheese in a crisscross pattern. Trim as needed to make the ends flush with the seam at the bottom of the cheese. Brush all over with a thin layer of the remaining egg mixture.

5 Bake for 25 to 35 minutes, until puffed and golden. Let cool for 10 minutes before serving with crackers. This baked cheese is also a great accompaniment for Salt & Burn the Bones (page 63).

FILED
Legacy

Salt & Burn the Bones

✦◊✦

YIELD **24** BREADSTICKS | TIME **2** HOURS **15** MINUTES PREP, **15** MINUTES BAKING

Can you really call it a witch hunt if you don't burn a few bones? Jericho town founder Joseph Crackstone didn't think so when he designed these tasty treats. Of course, this modified version of the original recipe doesn't use any actual witch femurs. Luckily you can get the same "plucked from the pyre" feel using breadsticks, blackened with activated charcoal and shaped to look like bones. They're salty and crispy, with a taste so good, you'll find yourself completely bewitched.

QUANTITY	INGREDIENT
1 teaspoon	pure maple syrup or honey
¾ cup	lukewarm water (90° to 100°F)
1 tablespoon	active dry yeast
1½ cups	all-purpose flour
½ cup	rye flour
1½ teaspoons	kosher salt
1 teaspoon	activated charcoal
½ teaspoon	dried rosemary, crushed
3 tablespoons plus 1 teaspoon	olive oil, plus more for the work surface

DIRECTIONS

1 Whisk together the maple syrup, water, and yeast in a measuring cup. Let sit for 5 to 10 minutes, until foamy.

2 Place the flours, salt, charcoal, rosemary, and 3 tablespoons olive oil in the bowl of a stand mixer fitted with a dough hook. Add the prepared yeast mixture and mix on low speed until a shaggy dough forms, 1 to 3 minutes. Increase the speed to medium and mix until smooth and slightly shiny, 7 to 10 minutes.

3 Drizzle 1 teaspoon olive oil over the dough. Turn to coat, then cover. Let proof for 60 to 90 minutes, until doubled in volume.

4 Line two half-sheet pans with parchment paper. Turn out the dough onto a lightly oiled work surface. Flatten into a 12 × 4-inch rectangle, then cut into four 12-inch-long strips. Divide each strip into 6 pieces, for a total of 24 pieces.

5 Roll out each piece of dough to a long snake-like shape about the width of a pencil. Each breadstick should measure between 12 and 18 inches long—it's very okay for them to be irregular in size and shape. Transfer the breadsticks to the prepared sheet pans, leaving about ½ inch of space between each one.

6 Cover the sheet pans with a clean kitchen towel and let the breadsticks rest for 15 to 20 minutes, until they look a bit puffy. Bake the breadsticks for 15 minutes, rotating the pans about halfway through to ensure even baking. Let cool in the pan for 10 minutes before carefully transferring to a wire rack to cool completely.

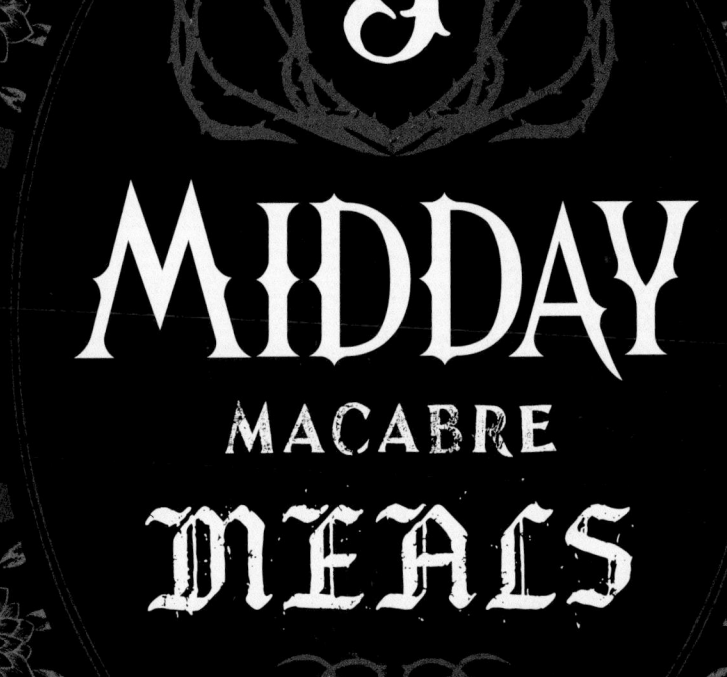

3

MIDDAY

MACABRE

MEALS

When the weather is nice, Nevermore Academy students like to go outside to the school's courtyard to eat in groups and share all the gruesome gossip of the day. While some cliques are more welcoming to all students, others prefer to stick to their own kind. And then there's Bianca Barclay, our resident queen bee, who wouldn't dream of lunching without her whole entourage in tow (though we can't be certain whether the utter devotion of her fan base is entirely organic or the result of a certain siren's song).

Either way, it's up to the Nevermore Academy Caf to serve a lunch buffet big enough to satisfy all our various cliques, no matter whom they hang out with. While we do serve normie staples like nuggets, pizza, and PB&J, we've decided to omit them from this cookbook as they're just too boring to bother with. Instead, we challenge you to try one of these clique-approved or legacy-acquired recipes at your next midday meal.

Our sophisticated Fangs love sipping on the cold Blood of My Enemies (page 74) gazpacho soup. Although you can make it entirely blood-free, they don't recommend it. Meanwhile, our Scales have been singing the praises of Life in a Fishbowl (page 78), a straight-from-the-sea sweet teriyaki salmon rice bowl. There are the mad-for-meat Furs who simply devour our Meat Me for Lunch (page 77). And don't look in the mirror now, but our Stoners love their Snake Hair Soup (page 83), made with udon noodles as slithery as their hairstyles.

We've also included some legacy recipes like Paint It Black Beans (page 84), which can be eaten alone or served alongside Boil Them in Oil Rice (page 127), a recipe you'll find in part 4. And Gomez Addams sent in his favorite sandwich recipe, the Croaked Monsieur Gates (page 87); yes, he named it after his former nemesis, and no, that doesn't mean he murdered him.

And we haven't forgotten Wednesday and Enid. Wednesday's Sloppy Woe recipe (page 68) is based on an old Uncle Fester favorite and can now be made without actually murdering anyone. Meanwhile, Enid chooses to go against the grain of her carnivorous kind by opting for All the Colors of the Grainbowl (page 71), a vegetarian lunch bursting with vibrant vegetables (which Wednesday insists Enid eat on her own side of the dorm room, lest the dish trigger her color allergy).

So the next time you start to feel sluggish (but don't feel up to cooking any actual slugs), skip the soggy sandwiches and try one of these macabre midday meals instead. While they may not make you fully wolf out, they'll at least be able to soothe your savage stomach until dinnertime.

Sloppy Wac

YIELD SERVES **4** TO **6** | **TIME 10** MINUTES PREP, **45** MINUTES COOKING

When I was a child, my Uncle Fester would sometimes come over to serve us lunch. His specialty was a meaty, messy sandwich he called Sloppy Joe. (It wasn't until much later I found the missing person poster for his friend Joe.) This version, often served in the Nevermore Academy cafeteria, is 100 percent Joe-free. Instead, the recipe uses ground beef and a tomato-based sauce, which you can substitute with blood when feeding Fangs.

QUANTITY	INGREDIENT
2 tablespoons	olive oil
1	small yellow onion, diced
1	large red bell pepper, stem and seeds removed, diced
1	celery stalk, diced
1 pound	ground beef
1 tablespoon	all-purpose flour
1 tablespoon	tomato paste
3	garlic cloves, minced
1 tablespoon	ancho chili powder
1 teaspoon	ground cumin
¼ teaspoon	ground cloves
¼ teaspoon	crushed red pepper flakes
1½ cups	tomato sauce
1 cup	low-sodium chicken stock
2 tablespoons	brown mustard
1½ tablespoons	lightly packed light brown sugar
1 tablespoon	apple cider vinegar
1 tablespoon	Worcestershire sauce
4 to 6	bulkie rolls or other sandwich rolls
4 to 6 tablespoons (½ to ¾ stick)	salted butter, softened
	Sliced American cheese (optional)

DIRECTIONS

1 Heat the olive oil in a large skillet over medium-high heat until shimmering (the oil will seem to move on its own). Add the onion, bell pepper, and celery and cook, stirring occasionally, until softened, 5 to 7 minutes.

2 Add the ground beef to the skillet and cook, using a wooden spoon to break apart the meat into very small pieces, until browned and cooked through, 10 to 12 minutes.

3 Add the flour, tomato paste, garlic, chili powder, cumin, cloves, and red pepper flakes. Cook, stirring constantly, until fragrant, 2 to 3 minutes. Stir in the tomato sauce, chicken stock, mustard, brown sugar, vinegar, and Worcestershire sauce. Bring to a boil, then reduce the heat to a simmer and cook, stirring occasionally, until the sauce is quite thick, 10 to 15 minutes. Remove from the heat and allow to cool slightly.

4 Split the bulkie rolls in half. Spread the butter evenly on the cut sides of each roll. Toast the rolls, cut side down, in a clean skillet or griddle over medium heat until golden brown, 5 to 7 minutes.

5 Distribute the meat sauce evenly among the buns and serve. If desired, top the meat sauce with a slice of American cheese.

FUN FACT: This recipe can also double as a crime scene if dumped on your dorm room floor. A perfect way to keep your roommate out while you're trying to work on your novel.

All the Colors of the Grainbowl

Don't tell my mom because she would get *so* growly, but sometimes I like veggie dishes. I know, I'm a Fur! I'm supposed to be carnivore to the core. But I recently discovered these grain bowls that are seriously the plant-based best. They're brighter than my hair, with purple and orange sweet potatoes, golden beets, red tomatoes, green kale, and colorful carrots. Which makes this dish as cute as it is yummy. And bonus—it's also healthy! Despite what my mother claims, veggies and grains are a huge part of the food pyramid. And yes, if you want, you can absolutely add your favorite protein. Chicken, salmon, steak—you do you!

QUANTITY	INGREDIENT
	DRESSING
½ cup	plain Greek yogurt (whole-milk, lowfat, or nonfat)
1	garlic clove
2 tablespoons	coarsely chopped fresh cilantro or parsley
2 tablespoons	coarsely chopped fresh tarragon or chervil
1 tablespoon	coarsely chopped fresh chives
1 tablespoon	lemon juice
2 teaspoons	honey
1 teaspoon	drained capers (optional)
½ teaspoon	kosher salt
½ teaspoon	freshly ground black pepper
	ASSEMBLY
4 ounces	kale, stems removed, chopped (4 cups)
1 tablespoon	olive oil
1 tablespoon	lemon juice
4 cups	hot cooked grains, such as quinoa, farro, or rice
1	large purple, orange, or yellow carrot, shredded
1 cup	halved multicolored grape tomatoes
½	roasted medium orange sweet potato (cubed or sliced into wedges; about 1 cup)
½	roasted medium purple sweet potato (cubed or sliced into wedges; about 1 cup)
1	roasted small golden beet (cubed or sliced into wedges; about 1 cup)
2 cups	shredded cooked protein of your choice, such as rotisserie chicken (optional)

DIRECTIONS

1 *Make the dressing:* Place the Greek yogurt, garlic, cilantro, tarragon, chives, lemon juice, honey, capers (if using), salt, and pepper in the bowl of a food processor and process until smooth, 2 to 3 minutes.

2 *Assemble the grain bowl:* Place the kale in a large bowl, then add the olive oil and lemon juice. Massage vigorously by hand until the leaves are softened, 2 to 3 minutes. Divide the kale evenly among four large salad bowls, filling one side of each bowl.

3 Add 1 cup of the cooked grain to each bowl, opposite the kale. Arrange the carrot, tomatoes, sweet potatoes, and beet in a rainbow shape along the top half of the bowl. Divide the cooked protein, if using, among each bowl, placing the protein in the center of the bowls. Serve with the prepared dressing on the side.

COOK'S NOTE: This is a great dish for using up leftovers, like the simmered chicken from Black Heart Chicken Breast (page 109), vegetables from Your Rainbow Roots Are Showing (page 95) or Snake Bites (page 124), or the meat from Give a Dog a Bone-In Rib Roast (page 103). Quantities can be adjusted based on what you have on hand.

Are You an Outcast?

Have you ever felt like you're different from everyone else?
That you don't belong with the normies of the world? Do you think you might
be an Outcast who would thrive at a school like Nevermore Academy?

Well, wonder no further. Our experts have developed a simple quiz to help you decide
if Nevermore Academy might be right for you.

- Have you ever felt feral on a night with a full moon?
- Have you ever wanted to sink your fangs into someone else's flesh?
- Have you ever accidentally sunk a ship just by singing a song?
- Does your bad hair day turn hairdressers to stone?
- Do you have vicious visions of the future that seem to come out of nowhere?
- Have you ever changed your shape to get out of a pop quiz?
- Do you turn into a murderous monster when someone else asks you to?

If you've answered yes to any of these questions, congratulations! You're an Outcast!
And while the rest of the world might consider you a freak of nature, we at Nevermore
Academy consider you family and encourage you to apply for admittance to our
academy for the next academic year.

Those of you who did not test positive, please don't despair. Historically, we've
found Outcasts come into their powers at their own pace and no two are alike, which
is why we welcome students from legacy families even if they haven't, for example,
fully wolfed out yet. As for the rest of you, keep up the faith. You never know when
you might freak out in the future.

The Blood of My Enemies

YIELD SERVES 4   TIME 10 MINUTES PREP, 4 HOURS CHILLING

FILE UNDER *Fangs*

Every Fang knows that revenge is a dish best served cold. And what better way to serve up those who wronged you than in a nice gazpacho? It's traditionally made with fresh blood, cucumbers, shallots, and oil (garlic optional), but you can substitute a tomato base if you don't have the blood of your enemies readily at hand. Either way, it's a great, refreshing taste of summer.

QUANTITY	INGREDIENT
1 pound	red heirloom tomatoes, cores removed and coarsely chopped (about 2½ cups)
1 slice	stale sourdough bread, torn into small pieces
1	large red bell pepper, stem and seeds removed, coarsely chopped
½	seedless cucumber, coarsely chopped
½	small shallot, coarsely chopped
½	Fresno chile, stem and seeds removed, coarsely chopped
1	garlic clove, quartered
4	large basil leaves
1 tablespoon	red wine vinegar
1 tablespoon	lemon juice
½ teaspoon	kosher salt
¼ teaspoon	freshly ground black pepper
3 tablespoons	olive oil, plus more for drizzling

DIRECTIONS

1 Place the tomatoes, bread, bell pepper, cucumber, shallot, chile, garlic, and basil leaves in a blender. Blend on low speed, gradually increasing to high speed, until smooth, 2 to 3 minutes.

2 With the blender running, add the vinegar, lemon juice, salt, and pepper. Drizzle in the olive oil. Season to taste with additional salt and pepper as needed. If a super-smooth consistency is desired, pour the soup through a fine-mesh strainer into a large airtight container, using a rubber spatula to help push it through. Cover with a tight-fitting lid. Discard the solids.

3 Transfer the soup to the fridge to chill for at least 4 hours before serving. When ready to serve, divide the soup among four bowls and drizzle with additional olive oil.

COOK'S NOTE: This is a great make-ahead dish since it requires so much time to chill. Make it up to 3 days in advance.

Meat Me for Lunch

YIELD SERVES **4**

TIME **30** MINUTES PREP,
50 TO **60** MINUTES COOKING

FILE UNDER
FURS

Imagine a stew so tasty that it leaves even alpha wolves speechless! This flavorful favorite, hailing from the Dominican Republic, is so juicy it will practically melt in your mouth. By slow-cooking pork in tomato sauce and spices, you'll end up with a meaty meal that can be served alongside rice, black beans, or tortillas. Bring this to the next potluck lunch and you'll be the most popular pup in the pack.

QUANTITY	INGREDIENT
2 tablespoons	olive oil, plus more as needed
1 pound	boneless pork chops, patted dry and cut into 1-inch cubes
1	large yellow onion, diced
1	large green or red bell pepper, stem and seeds removed, diced
1	serrano or jalapeño chile, stem removed, minced
6	garlic cloves, minced
1 teaspoon	ground cumin
1 teaspoon	ground coriander
½ teaspoon	Mexican oregano or marjoram
6	Roma tomatoes, cored and diced
	Kosher salt and freshly ground black pepper
1½ cups	low-sodium chicken stock
1 tablespoon	masa harina (optional)
1 tablespoon	coarsely chopped fresh cilantro
	Boil Them in Oil Rice (page 127), to serve
	Warm tortillas, to serve

DIRECTIONS

1 Heat the olive oil in a high-walled, 10-inch sauté pan over medium-high heat until shimmering (the oil will seem to move on its own). Add the pork in an even layer and let sit, undisturbed, until well browned on one side, 4 to 6 minutes. Continue cooking, stirring occasionally, until the pork is just barely cooked through, 3 to 5 minutes longer. Transfer to a clean plate and set aside.

2 Return the pan to the heat. Add the onion and bell pepper to the pan and cook, stirring occasionally and scraping up any browned bits from the bottom of the pan, until the onion has softened and is beginning to turn translucent, 8 to 10 minutes. If the pan looks dry at any point, add 1 tablespoon olive oil.

3 Add the serrano or jalapeño, garlic, cumin, coriander, and oregano and cook, stirring constantly, until fragrant, about 1 minute. Return the pork to the pan. Add the tomatoes and season with 1½ teaspoons salt and 1 teaspoon pepper. Cook, tossing and stirring occasionally, until the tomatoes begin to break down and release their juices, 5 to 7 minutes. Be sure to scrape up any browned bits as you cook.

4 Add the chicken stock and bring to a boil. Reduce to a simmer, cover the pan with the lid slightly askew, and let simmer, stirring occasionally, until the pork is fork tender and the sauce has thickened, 40 to 50 minutes.

5 If a thicker stew is desired, sprinkle and stir in the masa harina. Let simmer for 2 to 3 minutes longer. Season to taste with additional salt and pepper, and stir in the cilantro. Serve with the rice and warm tortillas alongside. Store leftover stew in an airtight container in the fridge for up to 5 days.

COOK'S NOTE: I'll often serve a smaller portion of this stew alongside a runny fried egg or two and some refried Paint It Black Beans (page 84) for a hearty breakfast. Be sure to serve with buttered toast or warm tortillas so you have something to mop up any sauce and runny yolk.

Life in a Fishbowl

YIELD   SERVES **4**   TIME **15** MINUTES

Being landlocked at Nevermore Academy can be enough to cause a poor sea siren to lose their song. And by lunchtime, they're longing to breathe in the salty air by the sea instead of the typical sweaty Stoner classroom stink. To help, we've created a protein bowl that's so seaworthy, it'll put even normies into a hypnotic trance. We have taken tender, flaky chunks of soy-glazed salmon and paired them with edamame and rice. One bite and you'll find yourself belting out sea shanties without care.

FILE UNDER

Scales

QUANTITY	INGREDIENT	DIRECTIONS
	EDAMAME	**1** *Make the edamame:* Bring 4 cups of water to a boil in a small pot over medium-high heat. Add the edamame and cook until just tender and bright green, 4 to 6 minutes. Drain the water and return the edamame to the pot. Toss with the sesame oil, salt, and shichimi. Set aside in a warm spot.
1 cup	frozen shelled edamame	
1 teaspoon	toasted sesame oil	
¼ teaspoon	kosher salt	
¼ teaspoon	shichimi togarashi	
	SAUCE	**2** *Make the teriyaki sauce:* Whisk together the soy sauce, sake, mirin, and brown sugar in a small microwave-safe bowl. Microwave for 20 seconds on high to warm through, then whisk again until the sugar dissolves. Set aside.
5 tablespoons	soy sauce	
2 tablespoons	sake	
2 tablespoons	mirin	
2 tablespoons	light brown sugar	
	SALMON	**3** *Make the salmon:* Season the salmon fillets all over with the salt and pepper. Heat the oil in a large skillet over medium-high heat until shimmering (the oil will seem to move on its own). Place the fillets, skin side down, in the skillet. Immediately reduce the heat to medium, then use two long spatulas to gently press the fillets down, keeping the skin in contact with the pan. Hold the fillets down like this for 1 minute, then allow them to cook, undisturbed, until the skin is crisp, 4 to 6 minutes.
4	skin-on salmon fillets (6 ounces each), patted dry	
1 teaspoon	kosher salt	
½ teaspoon	freshly ground black pepper	
1 tablespoon	neutral oil, such as canola or grapeseed	**4** Flip the fillets, then add the teriyaki sauce. Let the salmon simmer in the sauce until the sauce thickens slightly and an instant-read thermometer registers 130°F when inserted into the thickest part of the salmon, 2 to 4 minutes.
4 cups	cooked short-grain white rice, to serve	**5** Divide the rice among four bowls. Place a salmon fillet on top of each, flesh side down, and serve with the prepared edamame alongside.

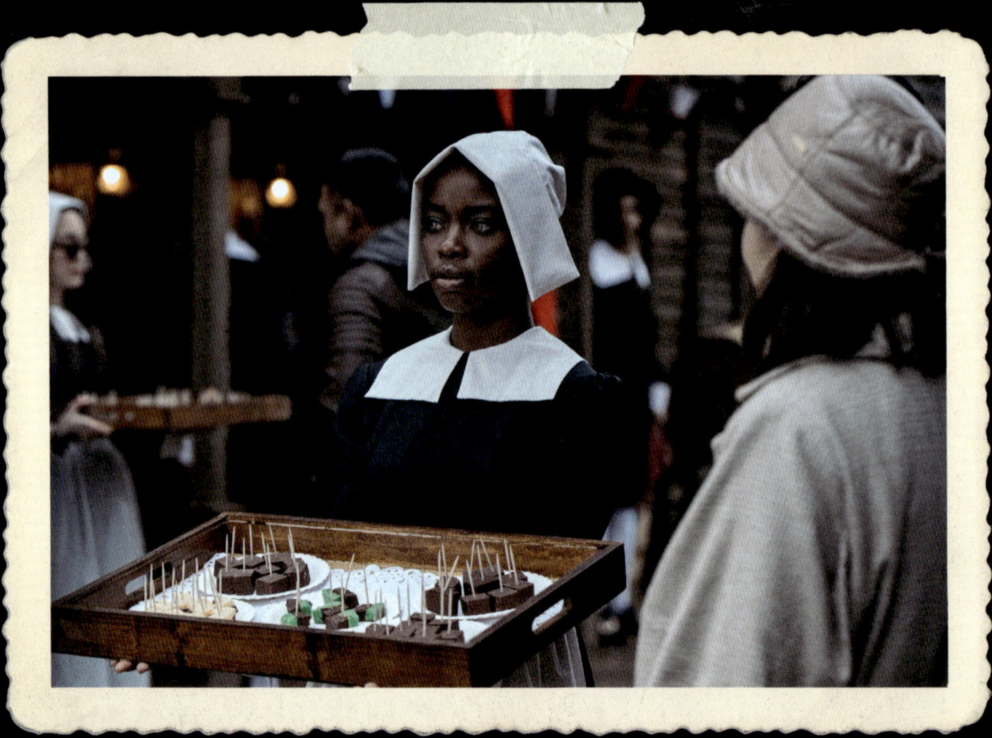

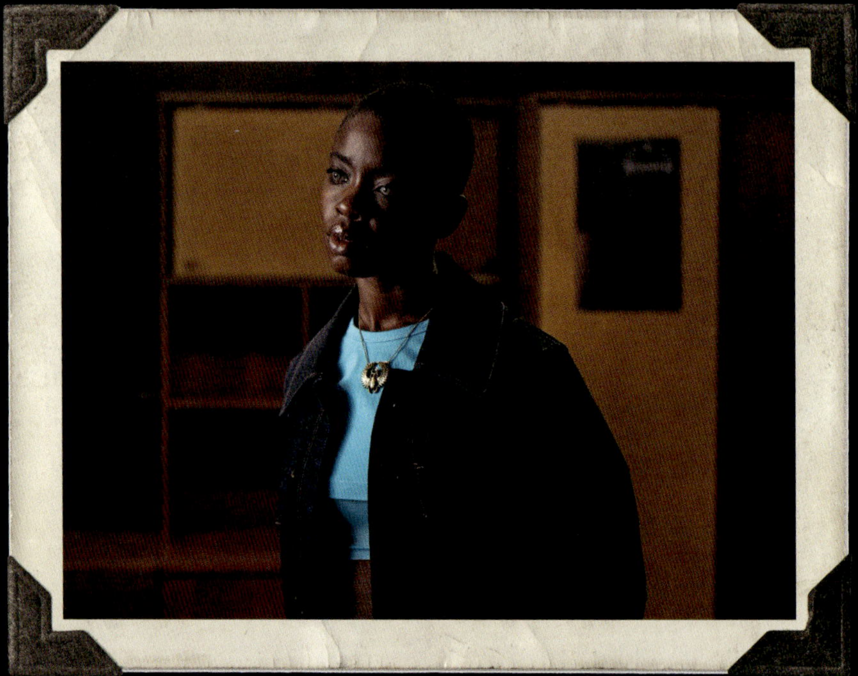

Snake Hair Soup

✦◇

YIELD **SERVES 4**   TIME **60 TO 70 MINUTES**

FILE UNDER

Stoners

Let's face it, gorgons aren't the most social of Outcasts. Can you blame them? Imagine going to a party, only to accidentally turn your sweetheart into stone. This soup is so good that even the shyest Stoner will want to share it. Made with udon noodles as smooth and slippery as a good hair day, it'll have your date practically hissing with delight.

QUANTITY	INGREDIENT	DIRECTIONS
	DASHI	**1** *Make the dashi:* Place the kombu and dried shiitake mushrooms in a medium pot. Add 6 cups of water and bring to a bare simmer over medium heat. Maintain the simmer for 30 minutes, taking care to skim off any foam that appears at the top. Using a slotted spoon, transfer the mushrooms to a small bowl and set aside to cool. Pour the dashi through a fine-mesh strainer into a large bowl. Set aside. Discard the kombu and any other solids. The dashi may be made up to 2 days in advance.
3 pieces	kombu (3 × 3 inches each)	
4	dried shiitake mushrooms	
¼ cup	soy sauce	
2 tablespoons	mirin	
1 tablespoon	sugar	
2	large carrots, cut into 1 × 2 × ¼-inch planks	**2** *Make the mushrooms:* Remove the stems from the fresh shiitake mushrooms, then thinly slice. If using a combination of mushrooms, coarsely chop the maitake and thinly slice the king oyster mushrooms. Mince the reserved rehydrated mushrooms.
1 16-ounce package	silken tofu, drained and diced	
3 tablespoons	white miso paste	
	MUSHROOMS	**3** Place all the mushrooms in a small saucepan and add the soy sauce, mirin, sugar, and ½ cup water. Bring to a simmer over medium heat and cook, stirring occasionally, until the mushrooms have reduced in size and absorbed most of the liquid, 10 to 15 minutes. Set aside in a warm spot.
12 ounces	wild fresh mushrooms, such as shiitake, maitake, and king oyster	
3 tablespoons	soy sauce	
1 tablespoon	mirin	**4** Pour the dashi into a large pot and bring it to a bare simmer over medium heat. Add the soy sauce, mirin, sugar, carrots, and tofu and continue simmering until the carrots are just crisp tender, 5 to 7 minutes.
2 teaspoons	sugar	
	NOODLES AND BOK CHOY	
24 to 28 ounces	frozen udon noodles	**5** *Meanwhile, make the noodles and bok choy:* Bring a large pot of water to a boil over high heat. Add the frozen udon noodles and cook according to package instructions. Transfer the noodles to four large soup bowls, leaving the boiling water in the pot. Blanch the bok choy in the water for 2 minutes, until bright green. Divide among the bowls.
8	baby bok choy, ends trimmed, halved	
	Shichimi togarashi, to serve	
	La-yu chili oil, to serve	**6** Dip a ladle into the dashi to remove about ½ cup. Add the miso paste to the ladle and stir until smooth. Stir this back into the dashi pot. Divide the soup and mushrooms among the bowls. Serve with shichimi and la-yu chili oil.

Paint It Black Beans

✦◦✦

| YIELD | SERVES 6 TO 8 | TIME | 10 MINUTES PREP, 3¼ HOURS COOKING |

Some women crave pickles and ice cream when they're pregnant. But when Wednesday was conceived, I found myself desiring these beans even more than being stretched on the rack while Gomez looks on (which was fortunate, since that activity is frowned upon for pregnant women). Day or night, side dish or main course, I had to have these dark, rich legumes stewed with onions, olive oil, and bay leaves. It's no wonder my little rain cloud was born with a heart as black as this dish (not to mention a severe color allergy)! Try this Addams Family staple by itself for lunch or pair it with Gomez's Black Heart Chicken Breast (page 109) at dinner. Sure to fill the black hole in your stomach every time!

QUANTITY	INGREDIENT	DIRECTIONS
1 tablespoon	olive oil	**1** Heat the olive oil over medium-high heat in a large Dutch oven until shimmering (the oil will seem to move on its own). Add the salt pork and cook, stirring occasionally, until the fat has rendered out and the meat begins to crisp, 10 to 12 minutes.
4 ounces	salt pork, or 4 thick slices bacon, diced	
1	small yellow onion, diced	
2	large carrots, diced	**2** Add the onion, carrots, celery, salt, and pepper and cook, stirring occasionally, until slightly softened, 5 to 7 minutes. Add the garlic and cook, stirring constantly, until fragrant, 1 minute.
4	celery stalks, diced	
2 teaspoons	kosher salt, plus more as needed	
1 teaspoon	freshly ground black pepper	**3** Add the black beans, chicken stock, and bay leaves. Bring to a boil, then reduce to a simmer. Cover and let cook, stirring very occasionally, for 3 hours, until the beans are tender and creamy. If the liquid level sinks too low, add more chicken stock as needed. Season to taste with additional salt if needed. Serve hot with crumbled cotija cheese and rice, if desired. Store leftover beans in an airtight container in the fridge for up to 1 week.
6	garlic cloves, finely chopped	
1 pound	dried black beans	
8 cups	low-sodium chicken stock, plus more if needed	
2	bay leaves	
	Crumbled cotija cheese, to serve	
	Boil Them in Oil Rice (page 127), to serve (optional)	

> "My appetite eludes me, Mother. The same way the truth eludes you."
>
> —WEDNESDAY ADDAMS

FOUNDED IN 1791   UNITAS EST INVICTA

Croaked Monsieur Gates

*❖*0*❖*0*❖*0*❖*0*❖*0*❖*0*❖*0*❖*0*❖*0 *❖* 0 *❖* 0 *❖*0*❖*0*❖*0*❖*0*❖*0*❖*0*❖*0*❖*0

YIELD **4** SANDWICHES | TIME **20** MINUTES PREP, **10** TO **15** MINUTES COOKING

It should be obvious that I don't suffer a stalker. Especially a normie who won't take no for an answer when it comes to my magnetic Morticia. I mean, I get it. She's worth every obsession, but you don't have to be a creep about it. Though I was proven innocent in the murder of Garrett Gates, I can't say I'm sorry he croaked. To celebrate his timely demise, Morticia and I christened our favorite sandwich in his name. A play on the traditional croque monsieur—which literally means "Mister Crunch," exactly the sound he made when falling from the terrace—it's a hot ham sandwich, smothered in cheese. As they say, revenge is sweet—or sometimes a savory sandwich.

QUANTITY	INGREDIENT
	BÉCHAMEL
1 tablespoon	unsalted butter
1 tablespoon	all-purpose flour
1 cup	whole milk
½ teaspoon	kosher salt
¼ teaspoon	freshly ground black pepper
	Pinch of ground nutmeg
	ASSEMBLY
2 tablespoons	salted butter, softened
8 slices	sourdough bread
	Coarse Dijon mustard
8 slices	deli ham, preferably Jambon de Paris
8 ounces	Gruyère, shredded (2 cups)

DIRECTIONS

1 *Make the béchamel:* Melt the butter over medium heat in a small saucier or saucepan (a saucier works well here—the rounded bottom makes whisking easier) until melted. Add the flour and cook, whisking constantly, until the raw flour smell disappears and the mixture smells slightly nutty.

2 Slowly pour the milk into the saucepan, whisking constantly and vigorously to ensure no lumps remain. Whisk in the salt, pepper, and nutmeg. Cook, whisking frequently, until smooth and thickened, 5 to 7 minutes. Set aside.

3 Place an oven rack in the upper third of the oven. Heat the oven to 425°F.

4 *While the oven heats, assemble the sandwiches:* Spread the butter on half the slices of bread. Place these slices, butter side down, on a bare half-sheet pan. Spread the mustard on the tops of these slices of bread, then spoon on 1 tablespoon of the prepared béchamel per slice.

5 Place 2 ham slices on top of each piece of the béchamel-covered bread. Sprinkle ¼ cup cheese over each sandwich. Top with the other 4 bread slices, pressing down slightly to compress the ingredients. Pour 3 tablespoons of the remaining béchamel onto each sandwich, followed by ¼ cup cheese.

6 Bake until browned and bubbling, 10 to 15 minutes. Allow to cool slightly before serving.

4

DINNERS

OF DARK

DESPAIR

Dinner at Nevermore Academy has always been served family-style to encourage cliques to branch out and try foods that might be outside their comfort zones, a practice that, over the years, has proved a massive success. Furs have found that fish can be quite flavorful, and Fangs can certainly appreciate a bloody rare steak. We also seat them by year rather than by clique to give students a chance to become better acquainted with their peers. In fact, some have become so well acquainted, they've chosen to take their friendships to the next level. But while we at Nevermore Academy will always appreciate a good love connection, we do insist students adhere to our policy of no hanky-panky at the dinner table, as our alumni Morticia and Gomez can attest.

It's also important to note that these days Nevermore Academy students are required to eat their dinners only in the cafeteria, a policy that was put into place after certain students were caught burying leftover bones in the floorboards "to gnaw on later." As you can imagine, this eventually produced a stink worse than an unwashed Stoner after gym class and forced us to put our foot down.

While some main and side dishes found in this part are your "typical Tuesday" fare, others can be served on more formal occasions—parties, date nights, funerals—whatever fun night you have planned.

For example, the Bloody Bolognese Bucatini (page 100) can be a quick and satisfying meal and great for carb-loading our track team the night before a big meet. It's favored by Fangs for its bloody appearance but also meaty enough to make a Fur drool. Uncle Fester's Famous Brain Roast (page 128), replacing an actual brain with a head of cauliflower, is both terrifying and tasty for "veggie-curious" students of all cliques. As is Enid's entry, Your Rainbow Roots Are Showing (page 95), a dish in which colorful vegetables are roasted together for maximum color and flavor. When perfectly plated, it's pretty enough for even a siren to appreciate.

For more special occasions, we suggest an Addams Family favorite, the Black Heart Chicken Breast (page 109). The mole poblano in this dish makes it both dark and delicious and perfect for a romantic, goth-themed date night. And for those of you looking for holiday flair, you might want to try the Blood-Glazed Turkey Breast (page 113) and all its terrifying trimmings: Edgar Allan Poe'tatoes (page 117), Blood Orange Cranberry Sauce (page 114), and Snake Bites (page 124), to name a few.

Whether you're planning a formal meal or just want to whip up something quick on a random Woeful Wednesday, these recipes have everything you need for a dark and delicious dinner—no matter your clique.

Like Lamb Shanks to the Slaughter

Imagine stewing your meat until it's so tender that it just falls off the bone. Of course, it takes time. Rush these lamb shanks and they'll be tougher than a Stoner who stared in the mirror. But slow cooked with red wine and tomatoes, they'll become as tender as a beautifully broken heart—and nearly as tasty. Plate the dish with a warm, creamy sand-colored polenta for maximum slasher-film-at-the-beach aesthetic.

QUANTITY	INGREDIENT
4 to 6	lamb shanks (1 pound each), excess fat trimmed
1 tablespoon	kosher salt
1½ teaspoons	freshly ground black pepper
2 tablespoons	olive oil
1	medium leek, white and light green parts only, rinsed and thinly sliced
2	large carrots, diced
3	celery stalks, diced
6	garlic cloves, minced
¼ teaspoon	ground cinnamon
	Pinch of ground cloves
1 cup	dry red wine
2 cups	low-sodium chicken stock
3 sprigs	thyme
1 sprig	rosemary
1	bay leaf
½ cup	dried cherries
4 tablespoons (½ stick)	cold unsalted butter, cubed
	Cooked polenta, to serve

DIRECTIONS

1 Pat the lamb shanks dry with paper towels. Season them all over with salt and pepper.

2 Heat the olive oil in a large Dutch oven over medium-high heat until shimmering (the oil will seem to move on its own). Working in batches, add the shanks and let them cook, undisturbed, for 5 minutes on each side until well browned all over. Set aside.

3 Add the leek, carrots, and celery to the pot. Cook, stirring frequently and scraping up browned bits, until softened, 8 to 10 minutes. Add the garlic, cinnamon, and cloves, and cook, stirring constantly, until fragrant, about 1 minute longer.

4 Pour in the red wine and let cook until the alcohol scent boils off and the wine has reduced slightly, 5 to 7 minutes. Scrape up any remaining browned bits from the bottom of the pot. Return the shanks to the pot. Add the chicken stock, thyme, rosemary, bay leaf, and cherries. Bring to a boil, then reduce to a simmer and cover.

5 Let the lamb shanks simmer until fork tender, basting and turning them every 20 minutes or so, for 1½ to 2 hours. Carefully transfer the shanks to a platter and cover with foil to keep warm.

6 Pour the cooking liquid through a fine-mesh strainer into a large heatproof bowl. Reserve the cherries but discard the rosemary and thyme stems and the bay leaves. Skim the fat off the top of the cooking liquid. Wipe out the Dutch oven with a paper towel and place it over medium-high heat. Return the cooking liquid to the Dutch oven and bring to a boil. Let the sauce cook, stirring occasionally, until reduced by about half and thickened.

7 Whisk the butter into the liquid to make a glossy sauce. Stir in the cherries. Return the lamb shanks to the Dutch oven. Toss to coat, then serve over polenta, along with the remaining sauce.

Your Rainbow Roots Are Showing

❖◇❖

YIELD **SERVES 4**   TIME **15** MINUTES PREP, **45** MINUTES COOKING

ILE UNDER

Enid

I know what you're thinking! Another veggie recipe from yours truly? But I'm sorry! There's nothing wrong with adding a little color to your carnage. Feel free to meat up all you want when you meet with the pack. But cross my claws and hope to die, sides are still a thing, and this one is seriously yum. Just channel your inner swine and you'll totally *dig* this roasted root vegetable medley. It's a perfect way to buck the pack mentality and let your freak flag fly.

QUANTITY	INGREDIENT
1	large orange sweet potato, peeled and cut into 1-inch cubes
2	medium golden beets, peeled and cut into 1-inch cubes
2 tablespoons	olive oil
2 teaspoons	kosher salt
1 teaspoon	freshly ground black pepper
2	medium purple sweet potatoes, peeled and cut into 1-inch cubes
2	medium red beets, peeled and cut into 1-inch cubes

DIRECTIONS

1 Arrange your oven racks so that one is in the upper third position and the other is in the lower third position. Heat the oven to 425°F.

2 Place the orange sweet potato in a large bowl. Toss with ½ tablespoon of the olive oil, ½ teaspoon of the kosher salt, and ¼ teaspoon of the pepper. Spread evenly onto one side of a half-sheet pan. Repeat with golden beets, and place on the other side of the half-sheet pan.

3 Using the same bowl, toss together the purple sweet potatoes with ½ tablespoon olive oil, ½ teaspoon salt, and ¼ teaspoon pepper. Spread evenly onto one side of a separate half-sheet pan. Repeat with red beets, and place on the other side of the half-sheet pan.

4 Roast for 20 minutes, stir and toss the vegetables on both pans, then swap the pans' positions to ensure even cooking. Roast for an additional 20 to 25 minutes, until the vegetables are easily pierced with a sharp knife or fork. Serve on a platter in chromatic order, starting with the red beets, then orange sweet potato, golden beets, and ending with the purple sweet potatoes.

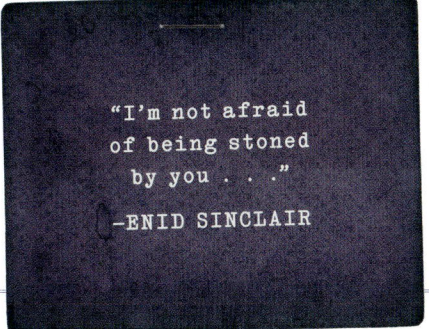

"I'm not afraid of being stoned by you . . ."

—ENID SINCLAIR

Frightening Fajitas

YIELD SERVES 4 TO 6   TIME 10 MINUTES PREP, 1 TO 6 HOURS RESTING, 30 MINUTES COOKING

My father used to sing a song about tortillas, until Mother told him it was too corny. But she never complained about his homemade chicken fajitas, which have more sizzle than my parents' love affair (and are a lot more appetizing at the dinner table!). He taught me to make the tortillas to go with them, using masa harina and his grandmother's old recipe. At first I'd burn the tortillas on purpose to make them black, which I felt was fair, since I was forced to tolerate the all-too-colorful red and green peppers that comprised the dish itself. But my family complained, and eventually I learned you can use activated charcoal to get the same effect, without the smoky aftertaste or your family's disapproval.

FILE UNDER
Wednesday

QUANTITY	INGREDIENT
¼ cup	olive oil, plus more for the pan
	Zest and juice of 3 limes
	Zest and juice of 2 oranges
2 teaspoons	ground cumin
2 teaspoons	kosher salt, plus more for peppers and onions
1 teaspoon	ground coriander
1 teaspoon	smoked paprika
½ teaspoon	ground black pepper, plus more for peppers and onions
½ teaspoon	Mexican oregano or marjoram
¼ teaspoon	ground chipotle powder or cayenne (optional)
2 pounds	boneless, skinless chicken thighs
3	medium bell peppers (green, yellow, and/or red), stems and seeds removed, cut into ¼-inch-wide batons
1	large white onion, halved and cut into ½-inch-thick slices

DIRECTIONS

1 Whisk the olive oil, lime zest and juice, orange zest and juice, cumin, salt, coriander, paprika, pepper, oregano, and chipotle powder (if using) together in a small bowl.

2 Place the chicken in a gallon-size plastic ziplock bag or a sealable container. Pour the olive oil mixture over the chicken, stirring to coat. Seal the bag or container, and refrigerate for at least 1 hour and up to 6 hours.

3 Remove the chicken from the marinade, shake off the excess, then gently pat dry with paper towels, but do not wipe all the seasoning off. Set the chicken aside on a clean plate.

4 Heat 2 tablespoons olive oil in a large skillet over medium-high heat until shimmering (the oil will seem to move on its own). Carefully lay half the chicken thighs in the skillet and let cook, undisturbed, until well seared and deep golden brown, 3 to 5 minutes. Flip the chicken over and cook for 3 to 5 minutes longer, until an instant-read thermometer registers 165°F when inserted into the thickest part of the thigh. Transfer the chicken to a clean plate, then repeat the process with the remaining chicken. If the pan looks dry, add more oil.

5 When all the chicken is removed to a plate, you may notice browned bits stuck to the bottom of the pan. Add the bell peppers and onion slices to the pan along with ¼ cup water, scraping up the browned bits, which will help flavor the vegetables. Cook, stirring occasionally, until the vegetables are softened and charred in some spots, 7 to 10 minutes. If the pan looks dry while cooking the peppers and onions, add another 1 to 2 tablespoons olive oil. Season to taste with salt and pepper, then remove the pan from the heat.

THE RECIPE CONTINUES THE RECIPE CONTINUES

QUANTITY	INGREDIENT (CONT.)
12 to 18	warm Black and White Tortillas (recipe follows), to serve
	Shredded Mexican cheese, sliced avocado, sour cream, or Soul-Sucking Salsa, to serve (optional)
	WHITE
1 cup	white masa harina
¾ cup plus 2 tablespoons	warm water, plus more as needed
¼ teaspoon	kosher salt
	BLACK
1 cup	white masa harina
1 teaspoon	activated charcoal
¾ cup plus 2 tablespoons	warm water, plus more as needed
¼ teaspoon	kosher salt

DIRECTIONS (CONT.)

6 Slice the chicken thighs into ½-inch-thick strips, then return to the pan with the peppers and onions. Toss to combine. Serve with warm corn tortillas and, if using, shredded cheese, sliced avocado, sour cream, or Soul-Sucking Salsa.

Black and White Tortillas

YIELD: 20 to 24 tortillas
TIME: 20 minutes prep, 25 minutes cooking (about 1 minute per tortilla)

1 *Make the white tortillas:* Place the masa, water, and salt in a stand mixer fitted with a paddle attachment. (Alternatively, you may use a handheld electric mixer or go ahead and get your hands dirty and mix by hand.) Mix on low speed until a smooth dough forms, 2 to 3 minutes. It should be soft and pliable but not sticky—like the texture of very soft clay. If it looks too crumbly, mix in more water, 1 teaspoon at a time, until you achieve the right texture.

2 Transfer the dough to a large bowl and cover tightly. Let sit for 10 minutes to allow the masa to fully hydrate.

3 *Make the black tortillas:* Stir together the masa harina and charcoal in a small bowl, then follow the dough-making instructions in steps 1 and 2.

4 Place a comal, steel or cast-iron skillet, or griddle over medium heat. Line a tortilla press with a quart-size plastic ziplock bag that has been split at the sides.

5 Shape a walnut-size piece of either masa dough into a ball. Place the dough ball in the tortilla press, just off center—the dough ball should be slightly closer to the hinge of the press. Close the press and press down firmly on the lever. Open the press, rotate the plastic bag 180 degrees, then close the tortilla press and lightly press down the lever.

6 Carefully peel the pressed tortilla dough from the plastic and gently lay it flat on the comal. Cook for 20 to 30 seconds, until the top has darkened slightly. Flip the tortilla with a thin spatula and cook for an additional 20 to 30 seconds, until both sides look dry. Transfer to a tortilla warmer or wrap in a clean kitchen towel. Repeat the process with the remaining dough. If working with a large griddle, you can get a rhythm going where you set a tortilla down to cook, press another, flip the first one, and so on. It takes some practice to get the timing down, but this is the fastest way to go.

COOK'S NOTE: Have some fun combining the dough to make half-and-half tortillas. Just use half as much dough to form 2 balls (start with the white to keep from transferring the charcoal to the white tortillas) of each color. Press them together, then carefully roll into a larger ball. Proceed with the pressing and cooking process.

Bloody Bolognese Bucatini

✦○✦

YIELD SERVES 4 TO 6 | TIME 60 MINUTES PREP, 3½ HOURS COOKING

While we're known for our bloodsucking, sometimes we rise from the coffin perfectly ravenous for a solid bite. This dinner recipe has everything a vamp could want to sink their fangs into: a bloody sauce (modified here with a tomato base), sautéed with whatever ground meat you might have lying around in your crypt. Serve it over hollow bucatini pasta and pair with a nice O-negative for a bloody delicious dinner.

QUANTITY	INGREDIENT
1 tablespoon	olive oil
1 pound	ground lamb or beef
2 tablespoons	unsalted butter
1	small yellow onion, minced
2	celery stalks, minced
1	large carrot, minced
	Kosher salt and freshly ground black pepper
1 cup	dry white wine or low-sodium chicken stock
1 cup	whole milk
1 28-ounce can	whole peeled plum tomatoes
½ cup	low-sodium chicken stock or water, as needed
1 pound	dry bucatini
	Freshly grated Parmesan, to serve

DIRECTIONS

1 Heat the olive oil in a large Dutch oven over medium-high heat until shimmering (the oil will seem to move on its own). Add the ground meat and cook, breaking apart with a wooden spoon, until well browned and cooked through, 15 minutes. Drain off any excess fat, leaving about 1 tablespoon in the pot.

2 Return to the heat, then add the butter, onion, celery, carrot, 2 teaspoons salt, and ½ teaspoon pepper. Cook, stirring occasionally, until softened and the onion is turning translucent, 10 to 15 minutes.

3 Pour in the wine, scraping up any browned bits from the bottom of the Dutch oven, and let cook until the alcohol scent boils off, 3 to 5 minutes. Stir in the milk, then bring back to a boil. Reduce to a simmer and cook, stirring occasionally, until the liquid has almost entirely cooked off, 25 to 30 minutes.

4 Add the tomatoes and use a potato masher to break them apart. Stir and bring back to a bare simmer. Cover the Dutch oven, leaving the lid slightly askew. Let cook, stirring occasionally, for 3 hours (check the pot every 20 minutes or so). If the sauce becomes dry, add the chicken stock and continue cooking for the full time.

5 By the 3-hour mark, the sauce should be thick, with no liquid left, and the meat should be broken down into very, very small pieces. Set aside in a warm spot while you prepare the pasta.

6 Bring a large pot of water to a boil over high heat. Salt generously (about 1 teaspoon per cup of water). Add the bucatini and cook according to the package instructions (this should take 6 to 7 minutes for al dente). Drain the pasta, reserving about 1 cup of the pasta water. Transfer the hot pasta to the Dutch oven and add half the reserved cooking water. Stir the pasta into the sauce. If the sauce is too thick, add more of the reserved water. Season to taste with additional salt and pepper. Serve with Parmesan alongside.

Give a Dog a Bone-In Rib Roast

◆∘◆

YIELD SERVES 4 TO 6   TIME 70 MINUTES PREP, 2½ HOURS COOKING, 20 MINUTES RESTING

It can be tough sometimes when the whole pack comes home for the holidays, starving and ready to eat you out of house and den. But every mama Fur knows she can easily soothe her savage beasts by serving a good old-fashioned bone-in rib roast. Easy to prepare and large enough to serve the entire pack, a rib roast is guaranteed to get wolfed down with gusto, especially if served bloody rare. Don't forget to cut up the rib bones and pass them around for a satisfying after-dinner gnaw. Bone appétit!

FILE UNDER

FURS

QUANTITY	INGREDIENT
1	2- to 3-bone rib roast (4 to 6 pounds)
3	garlic cloves, very thinly sliced
1 sprig	rosemary
1½ tablespoons	kosher salt
1 tablespoon	freshly ground black pepper

DIRECTIONS

1 Poke the roast all over with a small, sharp knife. Slide a slice of garlic into each hole. Pierce the cut side of the roast with a long, thin knife. Thread the sprig of rosemary into the hole.

2 Massage the salt and pepper all over the surface of the roast. Place the roast, rib side down, on a half-sheet pan and let sit at room temperature for 1 hour.

3 Heat the oven to 450°F.

4 Cook the roast until very well browned, 30 minutes. Reduce the heat to 325°F and continue roasting until the internal temperature of the roast registers 125°F for medium-rare, 135°F for medium, or 145°F for medium-well on an instant-read thermometer, 1½ to 2 hours longer.

5 Transfer the roast to a large cutting board and lightly tent with foil to rest for 20 minutes before carving and serving. Store leftover beef in an airtight container in the fridge for up to 3 days.

COOK'S NOTE: The bones can be discarded or used to make a flavorful bone broth. Place them in a pot of cold water (just enough to cover the bones by a few inches), along with a tablespoon of black peppercorns, an onion, and a few carrots and stalks of celery. Simmer for 2 to 3 hours, then strain. Drink as is, or use as the base for a soup or stew, including Eyeball Soup (page 123).

> "You're looking a little anemic. Have you been eating enough red meat?"
>
> —ESTHER SINCLAIR (ENID'S MOM)

Don't Move a Mussel

✦•◇•✦•◇•✦•◇•✦•◇•✦•◇•✦•◇•✦•◇•✦•◇•✦•◇•✦•◇•✦•◇•✦•◇•✦•◇•✦•◇•✦

| YIELD | SERVES 4 | TIME 5 MINUTES PREP, 10 MINUTES COOKING |

It's tough to have scales, not to mention the endless beauty and grace that come with them. You never know whether someone actually likes you for you or if they've just fallen victim to your siren song. But serve this delectable dish on a date and it'll tip the scales in your favor. An East Asian twist on a Native American staple, these mussels are steamed in a miso-sake stock for a one-pan recipe that's quick and easy to prepare and contains a treasure trove of taste. Serve it with crusty bread and your date will be singing your praises evermore.

FILE UNDER

Scales

QUANTITY	INGREDIENT
2 pounds	mussels, scrubbed and beards removed
¼ cup	hot water
2 tablespoons	white miso paste
1 tablespoon	neutral oil, such as canola or grapeseed
1	2-inch piece fresh ginger, peeled and cut into matchsticks
4	scallions, white and light green parts only, thinly sliced
½ cup	sake
1 tablespoon	lemon juice
	Crusty bread, to serve

DIRECTIONS

1 Pick through the mussels to ensure they're fresh. Live mussels will open slightly and close as they sit, but you can be proactive in checking them. They should close when tapped lightly—if any don't close when tapped, discard them.

2 Mix together the water and miso paste in a small bowl until smooth. Set aside.

3 Heat the oil in a large pot over medium-high heat until shimmering (the oil will seem to move on its own). Add the ginger and scallions and cook until fragrant and the scallions soften slightly, 2 to 3 minutes.

4 Add the mussels, increase the heat to high, and gently toss to redistribute the ginger and scallions. Add the prepared miso and the sake and stir to combine. Cover and let cook for 2 minutes. Carefully scoop the mussels from the bottom to the top to distribute the stock—you'll notice that most of the mussels have opened already. Cover and continue steaming until all the mussels have opened, 2 to 4 minutes longer. Remove from the heat. Discard any mussels that haven't opened, then transfer to a large serving bowl. Drizzle with lemon juice and serve immediately with the crusty bread.

COOK'S NOTE: White miso paste is sweeter and more subtle than red or brown miso paste (the latter two are fermented for longer, causing the flavors to intensify). It pairs well with the mussels, which have their own natural sweetness and brininess—but feel free to experiment with other types of miso paste here.

"A siren can never change her scales."

—BIANCA BARCLAY

Black Heart Chicken Breast

◇

YIELD SERVES 4 TO 6 | TIME 60 MINUTES PREP, 2½ HOURS COOKING

It's no secret I'm madly in love with my wife, Tish. She's my dark lady, my eternal night, my forevermore. Oh, the torture it would be to spend even a single night without her by my side. To illustrate my eternal love and devotion, sometimes I like to prepare a special at-home date-night dish—as dark and delectable as her heart. This mole poblano con pollo consists of a velvety mole sauce with a sweet hint of chocolate that's poured over chicken to produce a meal as rich, decadent, and delicious as my lady love.

QUANTITY	INGREDIENT	DIRECTIONS
2 to 3 pounds	bone-in, skin-on chicken breasts	**1** Place all the chicken parts in a large stockpot and add enough cold water to cover them by 3 to 4 inches. Add 1 tablespoon kosher salt and bring to a boil over high heat. Reduce to a simmer, cover, and let cook for 45 to 60 minutes, until the chicken is cooked through. Remove from the heat and keep in a warm spot—you'll use the stock in the mole.
2 to 3 pounds	bone-in, skin-on chicken thighs or leg quarters	
	Kosher salt	
12	dried mulato chiles (see Cook's Note)	**2** Remove the stems from all the dried chiles. Remove the seeds, reserving ¼ cup of them. Place a large Dutch oven over medium-high heat and add the chiles. Toast, tossing occasionally, until fragrant and pliable, 2 to 3 minutes. Remove the Dutch oven from the heat, transfer the chiles to a medium heatproof bowl, and cover with the boiling water. Let steep for 15 minutes, until rehydrated and soft. Rinse the chiles under cold water and set aside. Taste the soaking liquid—if it's bitter, discard it. If it tastes pleasant, reserve 1 cup.
12	dried guajillo chiles	
6	dried pasilla negra chiles	
	Boiling water	
1	cinnamon stick, broken into pieces	
2	whole cloves	
1 teaspoon	black peppercorns	
½ teaspoon	whole aniseed	
½ teaspoon	coriander seeds	**3** Return the Dutch oven to the heat and toast the cinnamon stick, cloves, peppercorns, aniseed, and coriander seeds, stirring and tossing occasionally, until fragrant, 1 to 2 minutes. Transfer to a spice grinder or the bowl of a food processor, along with the bay leaf, oregano, and thyme. Grind until fine. Set aside.
1	bay leaf, crumbled	
1 teaspoon	Mexican oregano or marjoram	
½ teaspoon	dried thyme	
¼ cup	neutral oil, such as canola or grapeseed	
1	small yellow onion, coarsely chopped	
½ cup	raw almonds	

QUANTITY	INGREDIENT (CONT.)
½ cup	raw peanuts
½ cup	raw pumpkin seeds
¼ cup	raw sesame seeds
¼ cup	raisins
6	garlic cloves, coarsely chopped
4	Roma tomatoes, coarsely chopped
2	tomatillos, husked and coarsely chopped
½	very ripe plantain, coarsely chopped
2	corn tortillas, torn into small pieces
½	bolillo or baguette (or 2 ounces any crusty white bread), torn to small pieces (1½ cups)
3 ounces	Mexican or other dark chocolate, chopped
	Freshly ground black pepper
	Boil Them in Oil Rice (page 127), to serve
	Warm tortillas, to serve

4. Return the Dutch oven to the heat and add the oil. Let heat until shimmering (the oil will seem to move on its own), then add the onion, almonds, peanuts, pumpkin seeds, and sesame seeds. Cook, stirring frequently, until the onion is softened and the nuts and seeds are toasted and smell nutty, 5 to 7 minutes. Add the raisins, garlic, and spice mix, and cook, stirring constantly, until fragrant, about 1 minute.

5. Add the tomatoes, tomatillos, and plantain. Cook, stirring occasionally, until the tomatoes and tomatillos break down and become saucy, 10 to 12 minutes. Add the corn tortillas, bread, rehydrated chiles, 1 cup of the reserved soaking liquid (if using), and 4 cups of the chicken stock (if not using the soaking liquid, replace with an additional 1 cup chicken stock). Bring to a boil, then reduce to a simmer. Cover and let simmer for 1 hour. Remove from the heat and let cool slightly.

6. Use an immersion blender to blend until smooth. (If you don't have an immersion blender, blend in a standard blender in batches until smooth.) Pour the sauce through a fine-mesh strainer into a large bowl, using a rubber spatula to help push it through. Discard any solids. Rinse out the Dutch oven and then return the mole to the Dutch oven. Place over medium heat and bring back to a bare simmer.

7. Stir the chocolate into the sauce until smooth. Give the mole a taste and adjust the seasoning with additional salt and black pepper. If the sauce is too thick, thin it out with more chicken stock, stirring until smooth. It should be glossy and thick but pourable, like gravy.

8. Serve the mole over the simmered chicken, along with the rice and warm tortillas. Store any leftover mole in an airtight container in the fridge for up to 1 week or in the freezer for up to 2 months. If you have leftover chicken, that can be stored in an airtight container in the fridge for up to 3 days.

COOK'S NOTE: It's always best to use a variety of chiles in dishes like this—each adds its own flavor for a rich, complex final dish. All these chiles can typically be found in most Latin American markets and spice shops. They can also be found from many online retailers.

Did Pilgrims Eat Turkey?

It may come as a surprise that there is no record of turkey being served at the Pilgrims' first feast. Experts say it was more likely to have been deer. It wasn't until 1863 when Abraham Lincoln declared Thanksgiving a national holiday that turkey became part of our "traditional" Thanksgiving meal. Even more surprising is that those early Thanksgiving holidays had nothing to do with the Pilgrims. It wasn't until late in the nineteenth century that they were included in the tale. Up until then, Thanksgiving was simply a holiday designed for Americans to give thanks for all they had.

Blood-Glazed Turkey Breast

●◆●

YIELD   SERVES 4 TO 6 | TIME 15 MINUTES PREP, 4 TO 24 HOURS BRINING,

2 HOURS COOKING, 15 MINUTES RESTING

A Thanksgiving turkey has become as American as apple pie. And we at Nevermore Academy have always loved a good tradition. For those of you brave enough to mix things up a bit during your next fall feast, give this Thanksgiving turkey recipe with a nod to Nevermore Academy a try. The Furs love the fact that a turkey breast takes a lot less time to cook than an entire bird, and the Fangs appreciate the nod to their culture with the blood-red tinge, thanks to a maple-and-cranberry glaze. It's guaranteed to make your next Thanksgiving a little more torturous.

QUANTITY	INGREDIENT	DIRECTIONS
	TURKEY	**1** *Dry-brine the turkey:* Pat the turkey dry with paper towels. Season all over with the salt and pepper. Place on an oven-safe wire rack set inside of a half-sheet pan. Let sit, uncovered, in the fridge for at least 4 hours and up to 24 hours. This allows the salt to fully penetrate the meat, for a more flavorful final dish (it also helps the skin get extra crisp).
1	boneless, skin-on turkey breast (2 to 3 pounds)	
1 tablespoon	kosher salt	
1 teaspoon	freshly ground black pepper	
	GLAZE	**2** *Make the glaze:* Place the cranberries, cider, maple syrup, brown sugar, vinegar, rosemary, salt, and pepper in a medium saucepan over medium heat. Cook, stirring occasionally, until the cranberries break down and the sauce thickens to a honey-like consistency, 15 to 20 minutes. Pour the glaze through a fine-mesh strainer into a small heatproof bowl, using a rubber spatula to help push it through. Set aside to cool slightly. Discard the solids. Transfer the glaze to an airtight container and keep in the fridge until ready to use.
1 cup	fresh or frozen cranberries	
⅓ cup	apple cider	
¼ cup	pure maple syrup	
¼ cup	lightly packed light brown sugar	
½ teaspoon	apple cider vinegar	
1 sprig	rosemary	
½ teaspoon	kosher salt	**3** *Roast the turkey:* Heat the oven to 425°F. Remove the turkey from the fridge and pour ½ cup water into the bottom of the sheet pan. Roast the turkey until an instant-read thermometer registers 160°F when inserted into the center of the thickest part of the meat, 75 to 90 minutes (the total time will vary depending on the size of the turkey breast). For the last 25 minutes of cooking, brush the turkey breast liberally with the prepared glaze every 3 to 5 minutes. When done cooking, loosely tent a sheet of foil over the turkey breast and let it rest in a warm spot for 15 minutes before slicing. Serve with unused glaze.
¼ teaspoon	freshly ground black pepper	

Blood Orange Cranberry Sauce

✦◦✦

YIELD **2½** CUPS | TIME **25** MINUTES COOKING, **20** MINUTES COOLING

For those of you masochistic enough to prefer your cranberry sauce from a can, you can stop reading now. But if you're hoping to elevate your holiday table and impress your guests, look no further than this Nevermore twist on your much-beloved normie Thanksgiving side dish. Instead of just boring old cranberries, this recipe adds blood oranges to the mix, which give the dish an intense color and a sweet, tangy taste. Serve it alongside the Blood-Glazed Turkey Breast (page 113) for a bloody good holiday meal that's beyond basic.

QUANTITY	INGREDIENT
12 ounces	fresh or frozen cranberries
	Zest and juice of 2 blood oranges
½ cup	granulated sugar
½ cup	lightly packed light brown sugar
1 teaspoon	ground cinnamon
¼ teaspoon	ground ginger
	Pinch of ground cloves
¼ teaspoon	kosher salt
½ teaspoon	rose water (optional) (see Cook's Note)

DIRECTIONS

1 Place the cranberries, blood orange zest and juice, both sugars, cinnamon, ginger, cloves, and salt in a medium saucepan. Bring to a boil over high heat, then reduce to a simmer.

2 Cook, stirring occasionally, until the cranberries burst and the sauce thickens, 15 to 20 minutes. Remove from the heat and stir in the rose water (if using). Let cool for at least 20 minutes before serving. Store leftover sauce in an airtight container in the fridge for up to 5 days.

COOK'S NOTE: The rose water here is optional but imparts a lovely floral flavor that pairs beautifully with the tart orange and cranberry flavors, bolstering their subtler notes.

Edgar Allan Poe'tatoes

YIELD SERVES 4 TO 6 | **TIME** 15 MINUTES PREP, 50 MINUTES COOKING

If you've been on the lookout for a good mashed potato recipe, look nevermore! This classic side dish comes from our most famous alumnus, Edgar Allan Poe, who found himself stuck at Nevermore Academy over the holiday break, when his pet raven took ill. Always one for the morbid and morose, Poe contented himself to stay in his room, until, one dreary midnight, he caught a telltale light coming from the kitchens. There he found other displaced classmates cooking up what they had dubbed a Freaksgiving feast. Poe was put on potato duty, and the result of his efforts are still celebrated at Nevermore Academy today. Creamy, rich pureed potatoes steeped in herbs, milk, cream, and butter. Truly a dream within a dream for your dinner.

QUANTITY	INGREDIENT
2 pounds	russet potatoes, peeled
	Kosher salt
½ cup	whole milk
½ cup	heavy cream
4 tablespoons (½ stick)	unsalted butter
2 sprigs	thyme
1 sprig	rosemary
1	bay leaf
	Freshly ground black pepper

DIRECTIONS

1 Place the potatoes in a large pot and add enough cold water to cover them by 4 inches. Season generously with salt. Bring to a boil over high heat, then reduce to a rapid simmer. Let cook until the potatoes are tender and easily pierced by a fork, 30 to 40 minutes. Drain the potatoes in a colander and let them sit for 5 minutes to allow any excess water to evaporate.

2 While the potatoes are cooking, add the milk, heavy cream, butter, thyme, rosemary, bay leaf, 1 teaspoon salt, and ½ teaspoon pepper to a small saucepan. Bring to a simmer, then cover and remove from the heat. Let the herbs steep in the milk mixture for 20 minutes, then pour the milk through a fine-mesh strainer into a small bowl and set aside. Discard the herbs.

3 Transfer the potatoes, one at a time, to a ricer or food mill and process them into a large heatproof bowl. (If you don't have a ricer or food mill, simply mash the potatoes slightly with a potato masher but not until smooth—overmixing the potatoes can make them gluey.)

4 Add about one-third of the milk mixture to the potatoes, then gently stir, allowing the potatoes to absorb the liquid. Repeat this process two more times until all the liquid has been absorbed and the potatoes are smooth and fluffy. Season to taste with additional salt and pepper, and serve.

DISTINGUISHED ALUMNI
Edgar Allan Poe

WE AT NEVERMORE Academy are proud to boast one of the premier poets and writers in the history of the world as one of our most distinguished alumni. In fact, Poe got inspiration for some of his works directly from our school, even writing a poem about our former raven mascot who spoke only one word, the name of our school, Nevermore. The poem went on to be such a success that we almost had to change the name of our institution, worried it might attract too much unwanted attention from the normie world.

Born in 1809 in Boston, Poe was a good student, our records indicate, known for his creepy and creative mind. He loved reading and writing tales of the macabre as well as canoeing on our lake. (He won the student cup so many times, they ended up naming it after him.)

He died tragically (and mysteriously) in 1849 at only forty years old. Today we at Nevermore Academy honor his legacy with a statue just outside our secret library.

THE EDGAR ALLAN POE CUP

Eyeball Soup

✦◇

YIELD SERVES 4 | **TIME** 20 MINUTES PREP, 30 MINUTES COOKING

FILED
Morticia

Marriage can be difficult, even for the most devoted couples like Gomez and myself, and it's important to keep the romance alive. For us, food is a love language, and on special occasions I like to mix up a cozy little comfort food I've dubbed Eyeball Soup to let mon cheri know I've still got eyes only for him. This traditional meatball soup has a simple soup base of onions, garlic, and tomato. Finished with meatballs, rice, and veggies, the soup will look like a vision and taste even better.

QUANTITY	INGREDIENT
1 pound	ground beef
1	large egg, beaten
1 tablespoon	chopped fresh cilantro
1 teaspoon	kosher salt
½ teaspoon	freshly ground black pepper
2 tablespoons	olive oil
1	small yellow onion, finely chopped
2	celery stalks, finely chopped
3 tablespoons	tomato paste
4	garlic cloves, minced
1 teaspoon	ground coriander
½ teaspoon	ground cumin
½ teaspoon	Mexican oregano or marjoram
3	medium carrots, cut into 1-inch pieces
2	medium Yukon Gold potatoes, cut into 1-inch pieces
8 cups	low-sodium chicken stock
1	bay leaf
	Lime wedges, to serve
	Boil Them in Oil Rice (page 127), to serve

DIRECTIONS

1 With clean hands, break apart the ground beef in a large bowl. Mix in the egg, cilantro, salt, and pepper until evenly distributed. Shape into 32 tablespoon-size meatballs (about ½ ounce each). Set aside.

2 Heat the olive oil in a large saucepan over medium-high heat until shimmering (the oil will seem to move on its own). Add the onion and celery and cook, stirring occasionally, until softened and just beginning to turn brown on the edges, 7 to 10 minutes. Stir in the tomato paste and cook, stirring constantly, until slightly darkened, 2 to 3 minutes longer.

3 Add the garlic, coriander, cumin, and oregano and cook, stirring constantly, until fragrant, about 1 minute. Add the carrots, potatoes, chicken stock, and bay leaf. Carefully add the meatballs. Bring to a boil, then reduce to a gentle simmer. Cover the pot with the lid slightly askew and let simmer for 10 minutes, undisturbed. Gently stir the pot, then continue simmering until the carrots and potatoes are tender and the meatballs are cooked through, 15 to 20 minutes.

4 Remove the bay leaf. Adjust the seasoning with additional salt. Serve with lime wedges and the rice alongside.

Snake Bites

✦✧✦✧✦✧✦✧✦✧✦✧✦✧✦✧✦✧✦✧✦✧✦✧✦✧✦✧✦✧✦✧✦

| YIELD | SERVES 4 | TIME 10 MINUTES PREP, 35 MINUTES COOKING |

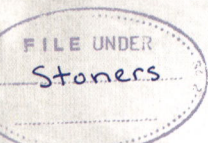

This side dish was so dubbed as part of an inside joke after some normie asked a Stoner on Outreach Day if they ever got a haircut. The Stoner was like, oh yes, totally, and promised to bring some of his snake clippings to the Weathervane the next day to prove it. That night he snuck into the Nevermore Academy kitchens, whipped up a batch of roasted parsnips, and cut them into small snake-like shapes. And the next day he showed them off to the normie, daring him to take a bite—saying they tasted just like chicken. The normie ran away screaming, which we all found *hiss*-terical. And to this day, these "snake bites" are served at the Nevermore Academy Caf with a side of chimichurri.

QUANTITY	INGREDIENT
2 pounds	parsnips, peeled and tops trimmed
2 tablespoons	olive oil
1 teaspoon	lemon zest
1 teaspoon	kosher salt
¼ teaspoon	freshly ground black pepper
½ teaspoon	dried thyme
½ teaspoon	dried oregano
	Pinch of crushed red pepper flakes

DIRECTIONS

1 Heat the oven to 400°F. Line a half-sheet pan with parchment paper and set aside.

2 Bring a large pot of water to a boil over high heat. Add the parsnips and cook until slightly softened, 5 to 7 minutes. Drain in a colander and let sit for 5 minutes to cool and dry slightly.

3 While the parsnips cool, whisk together the olive oil, lemon zest, salt, black pepper, thyme, oregano, and red pepper flakes in a large bowl. Add the parsnips and toss to coat.

4 Transfer the parsnips to the prepared sheet pan, spacing them evenly in a single layer. Roast until tender and golden, 30 to 35 minutes, flipping halfway through cooking. Serve hot or at room temperature. Store leftover parsnips in an airtight container in the fridge for up to 5 days. They also make a tasty, albeit not terribly colorful, addition to All the Colors of the Grainbowl (page 71).

Boil Them in Oil Rice

YIELD SERVES **8** | **TIME 15** MINUTES PREP, **30** MINUTES COOKING

When I was a child and got bored of putting my dolls on the rack, I'd go down to the kitchen, where I'd take out my torturous tendencies on dinner instead. Mother considered it cooking. I considered it practice. You never know, after all, when someone might need to be...persuaded. Case in point, this rice dish, which I toast and torture in boiling oil, then drown in a spiced tomato sauce, spiked with chicken stock. So satisfying to make and even more so to taste, especially when paired with my mother's famous Paint It Black Beans (page 84). One bite and you'll be ready to confess everything.

QUANTITY	INGREDIENT	DIRECTIONS
3 cups	low-sodium chicken stock	**1** Mix together the chicken stock, tomato sauce, cumin, salt, and pepper in a medium bowl. Set aside.
½ cup	tomato sauce	
1 teaspoon	ground cumin	**2** Heat the oil in a high-walled, 10-inch sauté pan over medium-high heat until shimmering (the oil will seem to move on its own). Add the rice and cook, stirring frequently, until all the rice grains are opaque, with some turning a toasty brown color, 5 to 7 minutes. Add the onion and garlic, and cook, stirring constantly, until fragrant, 1 to 2 minutes.
1 teaspoon	kosher salt	
½ teaspoon	freshly ground black pepper	
3 tablespoons	neutral oil, such as canola or grapeseed	
2 cups	long-grain white rice	**3** Carefully pour in the prepared chicken stock mixture—it will start to sputter and let off steam as soon as it hits the pan, so wear a kitchen glove or oven mitt and aim the liquid away from yourself as you pour. Bring to a boil, then reduce to a bare simmer and cover.
1	small yellow onion, finely chopped	
4	garlic cloves, finely chopped	
		4 Cook until all the liquid has been absorbed, 18 to 20 minutes, then remove from the heat. Let sit, covered and undisturbed, for an additional 10 minutes. Fluff the rice with a fork and serve. Store leftover rice in an airtight container in the fridge for up to 5 days.

"Just some light torture. Don't worry, I won't leave a mark."

—WEDNESDAY ADDAMS

Uncle Fester's Famous Brain Roast

| YIELD | SERVES 4 | TIME 15 MINUTES PREP, 45 TO 60 MINUTES COOKING |

My brother, Gomez, likes to constantly remind me that he got all the brains in the family. But that doesn't mean I can't enjoy brains from time to time at dinner. Since the genuine article can be tough to find, and tends to turn out a bit soggy, I've smartly switched to a vegetarian alternative that is so real-looking, it'll blow your mind. Take a whole head of cauliflower to serve as a brain, then roast it in the oven to get the neurons firing. Cover it with a tangy pink yogurt sauce for proper color and consistency and you'll end up with a dish that's grotesque and gluten-free! Which makes it a total no-brainer side dish for your next Halloween feast or plain old Tuesday treat.

QUANTITY	INGREDIENT	DIRECTIONS
	CAULIFLOWER	**1** *Make the cauliflower:* Heat the oven to 400°F. Whisk together the hot water and honey in a small bowl until the honey dissolves. Whisk in the olive oil, za'atar, salt, and black pepper. Place the cauliflower, upside down, in a large ovenproof skillet. Pour half this mixture all over the bottom of the cauliflower, letting it drip onto the undersides of all the florets for about 1 minute.
1 tablespoon	hot water	
1 teaspoon	honey	
2 tablespoons	olive oil	
1 tablespoon	za'atar	
1 teaspoon	kosher salt	
½ teaspoon	freshly ground black pepper	
1	large head of cauliflower, outer leaves and stem trimmed	**2** Flip the cauliflower over and brush the remaining seasoning sauce all over the top. Roast until the very center of the cauliflower is easily pierced with a sharp knife, 45 to 60 minutes.
	DRESSING	**3** *While the cauliflower roasts, make the dressing:* Place the beet, yogurt, garlic, shallot, lemon zest and juice, olive oil, honey, and salt in the bowl of a food processor. Process until smooth, 2 to 3 minutes. Transfer to a small bowl.
1	small red beet, peeled and diced	
1 cup	plain Greek yogurt (whole milk, lowfat, or nonfat)	
1	garlic clove, chopped	**4** Carefully transfer the roasted cauliflower to a serving dish. Drizzle some of the dressing over the top with, if using, a sprinkle of pink pepper. Serve with the remaining sauce alongside.
1 tablespoon	minced shallot	
	Zest and juice of 1 lemon	
3 tablespoons	olive oil	
2 teaspoons	honey	
¾ teaspoon	kosher salt	
	Freshly ground pink pepper, to serve (optional)	

"Monsters, murder, mayhem— what fun!"

—UNCLE FESTER

DINNERS OF DARK DESPAIR

5

DEVILISH DESSERTS

As normie American president Harry Truman once said, "There's nothing better than cake but more cake." And the pastry chefs at Nevermore Academy take this creed very seriously when spinning up their sugary sweets. From cute and creepy cookies to heart-shaped cakes that bleed red, they will happily serve up a spellbinding spread of delectable and dark desserts—perfect for your next Halloween party or a simple after-dinner treat.

First up: cakes. As Enid's been known to say, "Everyone deserves to be celebrated on their birthday." Even though Wednesday has repeatedly insisted she'd prefer "to be vilified" instead, the Nightshade Society, with the help of the Nevermore Academy kitchen staff, decided to bake her a cake. But not just any cake, mind you. Like our little rain cloud, this cake is as dark as the sky at midnight during a storm, making it completely hypoallergenic for those allergic to color.

Wednesday isn't the only one to have a special Nevermore Academy cake. Enid's Color Explosion Cake (page 139) sounds like a gender-reveal party gone bad but has a surprise that'll send you over the rainbow. Bursting with color and filled with rainbow-colored candies that spill out at first cut, this dessert is perfect for those who prefer life with a little added sparkle.

Other cliques also have favorite cakes, like the Fangs' beloved Bleeding Heart Cake (page 142), mini chocolate cakes with an oozing red center, perfect for letting your loved one know your heart bleeds only for them. Then there's the Rave to the Grave Cake (page 145), which is a joint effort between various cliques. Start with an ordinary sheet cake, then decorate it to look like an actual graveyard, complete with Headstones of Horrors (page 148), Goody's Ghost (page 170), and bone-shaped sugar sprinkles. So gruesome, you might forget it's edible.

But cakes are only the beginning of our repertoire. If you're craving cookies, you might try the above-mentioned Headstones of Horrors, shortbread cookies that can be personalized with your own RIP. Or maybe you'd like Eugene's Buzzworthy Biscuits (page 154), sweetened with local honey straight from the Hummers' hives. Or try Uncle Fester's Scout's Honor Cookies (page 158), which we're told taste similar to a certain caramel cookie favored by real scouts.

Other desserts include Sirens in the Black Sea (page 151), a Thai pudding; the perfectly purple and black Nightshade Society Poe Parfait (page 163); and As Jericho as Apple Pie (page 167), a taste of tradition modeled after that town's famous apple custard pie—the perfect finish for any Freaksgiving Feast (see page 210).

Note: While some might try to shame you into believing that these dark-themed desserts (like anything pumpkin spice) are suitable only during the Halloween season, we at Nevermore Academy hereby give you permission to trick-or-treat yourself at any time of the year. Unlike wearing white after Labor Day, scary is always in style and can be incorporated into baby showers, weddings, your best friend's babysitter's exorcism, or even a cozy night on the couch, bingeing Netflix.

Allergic to Color Cake

YIELD ONE **8**-INCH CAKE • TIME **60** MINUTES PREP, **45** MINUTES BAKING, **4** HOURS COOLING/CHILLING

FILE UNDER *Wednesday*

While I have no issue turning a year older, I do take offense when people throw parties supposedly in my honor as an excuse to gorge themselves on cake. But if you insist on observing this inevitable passage of time that has nothing to do with any personal achievement of my own, at least have the respect to serve this pitch-black cake for the occasion. It's charmingly void of color inside and out, reminding us of the everlasting emptiness we can all look forward to once we shed this mortal coil. The finished product can be decorated as dark as you desire with cobwebs, coffins, or cake toppers of esteemed dead poets. Just please don't allow Enid to put pink balloons in their hands.

QUANTITY	INGREDIENT
	CRÈME PÂTISSIÈRE
¼ cup	black cocoa powder
5 tablespoons	cornstarch
¾ cup	sugar
¼ teaspoon	kosher salt
5	large egg yolks
1 cup	heavy cream
1 cup	whole milk
2 ounces	dark chocolate, chopped
2 tablespoons	unsalted butter, cubed
1 tablespoon	vanilla extract

DIRECTIONS

1 *Make the crème pâtissière:* Whisk together the cocoa powder, cornstarch, sugar, and salt in a medium saucier or saucepan (a saucier works well here—the rounded bottom makes whisking easier). Whisk in the yolks, heavy cream, and milk until smooth.

2 Cook over medium heat, whisking constantly, until the mixture has thickened and begins to bubble, 8 to 10 minutes. At the 8-minute mark, slow your whisking speed and watch for bubbling—the moment you see the first bubble, set a timer for 1 minute and whisk constantly. Once the timer goes off, remove from the heat.

3 Place the dark chocolate and butter in a medium bowl. Pour the still-hot crème pâtissière through a fine-mesh strainer into the bowl with the chocolate and butter, using a rubber spatula to help push it through. Discard any solids. Let sit for 1 minute.

4 Add the vanilla to the crème pâtissière and whisk until smooth. Cover with plastic wrap, pressing the plastic onto the surface of the crème pâtissière. Let cool slightly, then transfer to the fridge to chill for at least 4 hours.

> "I haven't always been against birthdays. Each one reminds me I'm a year closer to death's cold embrace."
>
> —WEDNESDAY ADDAMS

THE RECIPE CONTINUES

QUANTITY	INGREDIENT (CONT.)
	CAKE
	Nonstick cooking spray
½ cup	black cocoa powder
¼ cup	Dutch process cocoa powder, plus more for the pan
½ cup	hot coffee
2 cups	all-purpose flour
1¼ teaspoons	baking soda
1 teaspoon	baking powder
1 teaspoon	kosher salt
2	large eggs, room temperature
¾ cup	buttermilk, room temperature
¼ cup	neutral oil, such as canola or grapeseed
1 tablespoon	vanilla extract
2 cups	lightly packed light brown sugar
	FROSTING AND ASSEMBLY
12 ounces	semisweet chocolate
12 tablespoons (1½ sticks)	unsalted butter, cubed
½ cup	hot water
2 tablespoons	golden syrup, honey, or corn syrup
1 tablespoon	vanilla extract
¼ teaspoon	kosher salt
½ teaspoon	black gel food coloring
¼ cup	black sugar sprinkles

5 *Make the cake:* Heat the oven to 350°F. Grease two 8-inch round cake pans with cooking spray, and line the bottoms with parchment rounds. Lightly grease the rounds. Set aside.

6 Whisk together the black and Dutch process cocoa powders in a small bowl with the hot coffee until smooth. Let cool to room temperature. Whisk together the flour, baking soda, baking powder, and salt in a medium bowl.

7 Place the eggs, buttermilk, oil, vanilla, and brown sugar in the bowl of a stand mixer fitted with a paddle attachment. Beat on medium speed until smooth, 2 to 3 minutes. Add the cocoa mixture and beat until smooth, 2 to 3 minutes.

8 Reduce the mixer speed to low. Add in the flour mixture and mix until just incorporated and no dry flour remains, stopping the mixer and scraping down the paddle and sides of the bowl as needed.

9 Divide the batter evenly between the prepared cake pans. Bake until a toothpick or cake tester inserted into the center of the cake comes out with a few moist crumbs clinging to it, 30 to 35 minutes. Let the cakes cool in the pans for 10 minutes before carefully turning out onto a wire rack to cool completely.

10 *While the cake is in the oven, make the frosting:* Place the semisweet chocolate and butter in a medium heatproof bowl over a small saucepan of simmering water (be sure the bottom of the bowl isn't touching the water). Melt the chocolate and butter together, stirring frequently, until smooth. Set aside to cool slightly.

11 Add the hot water, golden syrup, vanilla, salt, and food coloring to the chocolate mixture. Whisk to combine. At this point, you'll notice some separation, and the frosting will look curdled and broken—this is normal. Let the frosting sit at room temperature for 1½ to 2 hours while the cake cools, stirring every 20 minutes or so, until smooth and spreadable.

12 *Assemble the cake:* If the cakes have domed, trim the tops off with a cake leveler or long, serrated knife. Then slice them in half horizontally to create 4 equal layers.

13 Choose the best-looking 3 layers for the cake. Transfer the trimmed tops and extra layer to a large bowl and break apart with your hands to fine crumbs.

14. Whisk the crème pâtissière until smooth. Transfer 1 layer of the cake to a cake stand or platter. Spread half the crème pâtissière over the top in an even layer. Place the second layer on top, then evenly spread the remaining crème pâtissière on top of that layer. Top with the final layer. Place the cake in the fridge to chill until the frosting is at room temperature.

15. When the frosting is ready, take the cake out of the fridge. Working quickly, spread about half the frosting all over the top and sides of the cake in a thin layer—don't worry about it looking perfect, especially on the sides. Return the cake to the fridge and chill until the frosting is set (it will go from glossy to matte), 10 to 15 minutes.

16. Take the cake out of the fridge and spread the remaining frosting over the top and sides of the cake, making sure the top is as smooth and level as possible. Again, it's okay if the sides are imperfect because they are about to be covered: Press an even layer of the reserved cake crumbs all over the sides of the cake. Decorate the top of the cake with black sugar sprinkles. Keep in a cool place or chilled in the fridge until ready to serve. This cake is best eaten within 24 hours, but you can tightly wrap leftovers in plastic wrap and store in the fridge for up to 3 days.

"Please excuse Wednesday. She's allergic to color."

—MORTICIA ADDAMS

Color Explosion Cake

✦◇

YIELD ONE **8**-INCH CAKE │ TIME **60** MINUTES PREP, **30** MINUTES BAKING

FILE UNDER

Enid

I adore birthdays. Well, at least other people's birthdays. But that's only because my mother would use my birthday as an excuse to once again nag me on why I hadn't wolfed out yet and to offer unwelcome gift vouchers for lycanthropy conversion summer camps. But other people's birthdays? I use them as an excuse to make my absolute favorite birthday cake *ever*. Consider it an anti-Wednesday cake because, unlike my color-allergic roommate, this one practically explodes with color (I mean, not literally—though Wednesday would probably prefer it if it did). It starts with this beautiful tiered layer cake decorated with multi-colored frosting. Then, when you cut it open? Surprise! Candy starts spilling out in all the colors of the rainbow. It's as fun and festive as my fingernails!

QUANTITY	INGREDIENT	DIRECTIONS
	CAKE	**1** *Make the cake:* Heat the oven to 325°F. Grease three 8-inch round cake pans with cooking spray, and line the bottoms with parchment rounds. Lightly grease the rounds. Set aside.
	Nonstick cooking spray	
3 cups	cake flour	
2 teaspoons	baking powder	**2** Whisk together the cake flour, baking powder, baking soda, and salt in a medium bowl. Set aside.
½ teaspoon	baking soda	
½ teaspoon	kosher salt	**3** Place the butter, oil, and sugar in the bowl of a stand mixer fitted with a paddle attachment. Beat on medium speed until smooth and creamy, 3 to 5 minutes. The mixture doesn't need to be light and fluffy. With the mixer running, beat in the egg until incorporated, 1 to 2 minutes.
12 tablespoons (1½ sticks)	unsalted butter, softened	
2 tablespoons	neutral oil, such as canola or grapeseed	
1¼ cups	sugar	
1	large egg, room temperature	**4** Add the egg whites and vanilla, beating until incorporated. Stop the mixer to scrape down the paddle and sides and bottom of the bowl as needed. Beat on medium speed for 1 to 2 minutes longer, until smooth.
3	large egg whites, room temperature	
1 tablespoon	vanilla extract	**5** Reduce the mixer speed to low. Add one-third of the flour mixture and beat until just incorporated. Add half the buttermilk, beating until smooth. Repeat with the remaining flour and buttermilk, ending with the final one-third of the flour. Once the flour is incorporated, stop the mixer and scrape down the paddle and sides and bottom of the bowl, folding in any remaining dry flour.
1 cup	buttermilk, room temperature	
½ cup	rainbow sprinkles, plus more for filling and decorating	

6 Fold in the sprinkles. Divide the batter evenly among the three prepared cake pans, smoothing the top. Bake for 25 to 30 minutes, rotating the pans about halfway through, until a toothpick or cake tester inserted into the center of the cake comes out with a few moist crumbs clinging to it. Let the cakes cool in the pans for 10 minutes before carefully transferring to a wire rack to cool completely. While the cakes are baking, wash the mixer bowl to reuse for the frosting.

QUANTITY	INGREDIENT (CONT.)
	FROSTING AND ASSEMBLY
1 cup	sugar
¼ teaspoon	kosher salt
6	large egg whites
4 sticks	unsalted butter, cubed, room temperature
1 tablespoon	vanilla extract
½ cup	seedless raspberry jam
	Electric pink gel food coloring
	Red gel food coloring
	Orange gel food coloring
	Yellow gel food coloring
	Green gel food coloring
	Blue gel food coloring
	Purple gel food coloring
1 cup	rainbow-colored candy, such as candy-coated chocolate

> "Anytime I grow nauseous at the sight of a rainbow or hear a pop song that makes my ears bleed, I'll think of you."
>
> —WEDNESDAY ADDAMS

DIRECTIONS (CONT.)

7 *Make the frosting:* Place the sugar, salt, and egg whites in a large heatproof bowl (ideally your clean stand mixer bowl, but a separate bowl will work fine). Set the bowl over a medium saucepan of simmering water (be sure the bottom of the bowl isn't touching the water). Gently heat the mixture, whisking constantly, until the sugar dissolves and the mixture reaches 150°F, as measured using a candy thermometer or instant-read thermometer. Remove from the heat.

8 If you used a separate bowl, transfer the egg white mixture to the clean, dry bowl of your stand mixer fitted with a whisk attachment. Whisk on medium speed until foamy, then increase the speed to medium-high. Beat until stiff, glossy peaks form, 10 to 15 minutes. Take the temperature of the meringue—it should be room temperature by the time you're finished (70° to 72°F).

9 Reduce the mixer speed to medium and add the butter, a few tablespoons at a time, waiting for the butter to be incorporated before adding more. The mixture may look soupy about halfway through, but keep adding the butter until it's all completely incorporated. Whisk in the vanilla. Remove about 2 cups of the frosting and set aside.

10 With the mixer running, add the raspberry jam 1 tablespoon at a time until it's fully incorporated. The frosting will look pale pink. Add a few drops, or up to ½ teaspoon, of electric pink gel food coloring until the frosting turns bright pink. Set aside.

11 Divide the reserved frosting among six small bowls (about ⅓ cup per bowl). Color each bowl of frosting with each of the gel food colorings to make red, orange, yellow, green, blue, and purple frosting. You should need only a few drops per bowl, or up to ¼ teaspoon, depending on the strength of your food coloring.

12 Transfer the six colored frostings to six small piping bags, one color per bag. Lay a sheet of plastic wrap flat on a clean work surface. Trim the tip off the red frosting bag to create a 1-inch opening. Starting about 1 inch from the bottom of one long side of the plastic wrap, pipe a 1 × 1 inch-thick line of red frosting toward the other long side until the frosting is spent. Repeat the process using the remaining colors, piping each line of frosting directly up against the previous color in the following order: red, orange, yellow, green, blue, purple. The lines of frosting should be touching and roughly the same size.

13 Carefully lift the short side of the plastic wrap closest to the red frosting and roll the frosting up over itself to create one large rainbow log of frosting, rolling the plastic over the whole log. Gently roll the frosting log to seal the colors together, but be careful not to mix them.

14 Trim one short end of the plastic wrap off so the frosting is exposed. Fit a large star tip (or decorative tip of your choice) to a large piping bag. Carefully slide the rainbow frosting, plastic wrap and all, into the piping bag.

15 *Assemble the cake:* If the cakes have domed, trim the tops off with a cake leveler or long, serrated knife. Place 1 layer on a cake stand or large platter. Spread about ¾ cup of the raspberry buttercream over the top of the layer using an offset spatula. Using a sharp knife or a 4- to 5-inch circle cookie cutter, remove a 4- to 5-inch round from the center of the next layer. Stack the donut-shaped layer on top of the first layer.

16 Fill the hole in the center layer with the rainbow candy and additional rainbow sprinkles. Spread ½ cup of the raspberry buttercream over the top of the center layer, leaving the candy exposed. Top with the final layer of cake, and spread about half the remaining raspberry buttercream over the top and sides of the cake in a thin layer. Chill the cake for 15 minutes until the frosting is set.

17 Remove the cake from the fridge and spread the rest of the raspberry buttercream over the cake, ensuring that the top and sides are as smooth as possible. Finish frosting the cake by piping large rosettes or tall swirls of the rainbow frosting all around the top of the cake. Scatter rainbow sprinkles over the top and sides of the cake and serve. Tightly wrap leftover cake in plastic wrap and store in the fridge for 3 to 5 days. Let the cake come to room temperature before eating for the best flavor and texture.

Bleeding Heart Cake

✦◦✦◦✦◦✦◦✦◦✦◦✦◦✦◦✦◦✦◦✦◦✦◦✦◦✦◦✦◦✦◦✦◦✦◦✦◦✦

| YIELD **4** CAKES | TIME **15** MINUTES PREP, **14** MINUTES BAKING |

Fangs have two great loves: fresh blood and the endless night. In this recipe we combine the two to create a bloody delicious surprise for your loved one. On first glance, these individual cakes appear pink, delicious, and utterly inno-cent. It's not until you cut into one that it starts bleeding out all over your plate. Traditionally Fangs have used actual congealed blood for the filling, but molten ruby-red chocolate mixed with raspberries produces a similar look. Either way, we promise this dessert definitely does not suck.

FILE UNDER

Fangs

QUANTITY	INGREDIENT
6 tablespoons (¾ stick)	unsalted butter, cubed, plus more for the ramekins
2 tablespoons	all-purpose flour, plus more for the ramekins
6 ounces	ruby chocolate chips or coarsely chopped ruby chocolate
2	large eggs
2	large egg yolks
¼ teaspoon	kosher salt
1 tablespoon	freeze-dried raspberry powder, plus more for dusting
3 drops	red gel food coloring
8	fresh raspberries

COOK'S NOTE: As the raspberries cook down and mix with the batter, they'll give the cake a molten blood-red center that gushes out when you cut into it. However, it's important to serve these cakes hot, or the center will set and you'll lose the gushing effect (though they'll still be tasty).

DIRECTIONS

1 Heat the oven to 450°F. Grease four 6-ounce ramekins generously with butter. Place about 1 teaspoon flour in each ramekin, then rotate the ramekins on their sides to coat the bottom and sides with flour. Tap out the excess—the inside of the ramekins should be very lightly dusted with flour. Place the ramekins on a half-sheet pan and set aside.

2 Place the chocolate and the 6 tablespoons butter in a medium heatproof bowl over a small pot of barely simmering water (be sure the bottom of the bowl isn't touching the water). Melt the chocolate and butter together, stirring frequently, until smooth. Set aside to cool slightly.

3 Place the eggs, egg yolks, and salt in the bowl of a stand mixer fitted with a whisk attachment and beat on medium-high speed until thick and pale, 5 to 7 minutes. (Alternatively, you can place these ingredients in a medium bowl and beat with a handheld mixer.)

4 Fold the chocolate mixture into the eggs until smooth. Sift in the flour and the raspberry powder. Add the red gel food coloring and fold until smooth and fully incorporated.

5 Divide the batter among the ramekins. Press 2 raspberries into each ramekin until just covered by the batter. Bake for 12 to 14 minutes, until the edges of the cake are set, but the centers are still wobbly.

6 Let the cakes sit, undisturbed, for 2 minutes. Top each ramekin with a small plate, then invert. Let sit for 10 to 15 seconds, until the cakes release themselves from the ramekins. Dust with additional raspberry powder and serve immediately.

Rave to the Grave Cake

✦◦✦

YIELD ONE 9 × 13-INCH CAKE   TIME 60 MINUTES PREP, 30 MINUTES
BAKING, 4 HOURS COOLING

While usually we canines prefer carnage to cake, this particular recipe can be a great addition to your next family howl-o-day. A simple chocolate cake, covered in steak tartare (or chocolate frosting) is cleverly topped with a "graveyard rave under a full moon" scene, which we all know is the perfect place to wolf out with our friends. Decorated with cookie crumbs for dirt, bone candy sprinkles (or real bones, your choice!), or shortbread headstones to memorialize any unfortunate hydes who dared cross our paths, this cake is guaranteed to bring out the alpha in us all.

QUANTITY	INGREDIENT
	CAKE
	Nonstick cooking spray
1 cup	hot coffee
¾ cup	cocoa powder
2 sticks	unsalted butter
2 cups	all-purpose flour
1½ cups	granulated sugar
½ teaspoon	kosher salt
1½ teaspoons	baking soda
2	large eggs, room temperature
1 cup	buttermilk, room temperature
1 tablespoon	vanilla extract
	FROSTING AND ASSEMBLY
12 tablespoons (1½ sticks)	unsalted butter, softened
3 cups	powdered sugar
½ cup	cocoa powder
¼ teaspoon	kosher salt
3 tablespoons	heavy cream
2 teaspoons	vanilla extract
1 cup	chocolate cookie crumbs
	Headstones of Horrors (page 148)
	Goody's Ghost (page 170)
	Bone candy sprinkles (optional)

DIRECTIONS

1 *Make the cake:* Heat the oven to 350°F. Grease a 9 × 13-inch cake pan or glass baking dish with cooking spray. Set aside.

2 Whisk together the hot coffee and cocoa powder in a small bowl until smooth. Set aside to cool to room temperature.

3 Melt the butter in a medium saucepan over medium heat, swirling and stirring occasionally, until the solids just begin to turn golden brown, 5 to 7 minutes. Remove from the heat and let cool to room temperature.

4 Whisk together the flour, sugar, salt, and baking soda in a medium bowl. Whisk together the eggs, buttermilk, vanilla, and cocoa mixture in a large bowl until smooth. Add the flour mixture and stir until smooth.

5 Pour the cake batter into the prepared cake pan. Bake until a toothpick or cake tester inserted into the center of the cake comes out clean with a few moist crumbs clinging to it. Let cool in the pan to room temperature.

6 *Make the frosting:* Place the butter in the bowl of a stand mixer fitted with a paddle attachment. Beat on medium-high speed until creamy and lightened in color, 3 to 5 minutes.

7 Stop the mixer, add the powdered sugar, cocoa powder, salt, heavy cream, and vanilla, then resume mixing at the lowest setting until moistened through. Increase the speed to medium-high and continue beating, scraping down the paddle and sides and bottom of the bowl as needed, until completely smooth, light, and fluffy, 7 to 10 minutes.

QUANTITY	INGREDIENT	DIRECTIONS (CONT.)

8 Spread the frosting over the top of the cake in an even layer. Remove the cake from the pan. Use the back of a spoon to swoop and swirl the frosting to give it an irregular texture. Scatter the cookie crumbs over the top, then decorate with 4 to 8 each of the Headstones of Horrors and Goody's Ghost meringues, scattering a few bone candy sprinkles (if using) in front of each headstone-shaped cookie.

COOK'S NOTE: Feel free to embellish the decorations as you like! Perhaps a candy hand reaching from the dirt in front of a headstone or candy spiders crawling all over. You can also break some of the headstones to give a well-worn look to the graveyard. Dried edible flowers also make a fun addition with their wilted appearance.

Headstones of Horrors

❖

YIELD **1** DOZEN COOKIES | TIME **8.5** MINUTES PREP, **18** MINUTES BAKING

Here lies a Stoner who literally died of embarrassment after accidentally turning himself to stone and standing up his date! Now these and other troubling times when you and your friends have hit rock bottom can be hilariously memorialized on these special shortbread cookies, cut in the shapes of headstones. The addition of black sesame paste to the batter colors the stones with an on-brand gray hue and provides a nutty, toasty flavor that will rock your taste buds. Chow on one between classes or combine together to create your own cake-top graveyard scene.

FILE UNDER
Stoners

QUANTITY	INGREDIENT	DIRECTIONS
1¼ cups	all-purpose flour, plus more for the work surface	**1** Pulse the flour and butter together in the bowl of a food processor until the mixture resembles wet sand, 2 to 3 minutes. Add the sugar, salt, sesame paste, vanilla, and almond extract. Pulse the mixture until a smooth dough forms and clings to the blade, 3 to 5 minutes.
8 tablespoons (1 stick)	cold unsalted butter, cubed	
½ cup	sugar	**2** Shape the dough into a disc and wrap tightly with plastic wrap. Chill for 1 hour. Line a half-sheet pan with parchment paper.
¼ teaspoon	kosher salt	
2 tablespoons	black sesame paste	**3** Turn out the dough onto a lightly floured surface. Roll out the dough to a thickness of about ¼ inch. Use a headstone-shaped cookie cutter to punch out as many cookies as you can. Transfer to the prepared sheet pan, spacing them about 1 inch apart. Gather up the scraps of dough, reroll, and repeat the process until you have a dozen cookies. Place the pan in the freezer for 15 minutes.
1 teaspoon	vanilla extract	
Scant ¼ teaspoon	almond extract	
	White gel icing in a tube, for decorating	

4 Heat the oven to 350°F.

5 Bake the cookies for 15 to 18 minutes, until just beginning to turn golden at the edges. Let cool on the pan for 5 minutes, then transfer to a wire rack to cool completely. Use the white gel icing to decorate and write on the headstone cookies. These cookies can be enjoyed on their own or used as decorations for a Rave to the Grave Cake (page 145).

Sirens in the Black Sea

✦◦✦

| YIELD | SERVES 4 TO 6 | TIME | 90 MINUTES |

Imagine a lone ship, adrift at sea. Moonlight rippling on the dark water. And suddenly you hear the sweet sounds of the siren's song steering you off course with their haunting melody. This traditional Thai pudding will prove almost as alluring at your next dinner party. Made from forbidden black rice, this dessert has a natural inky color, a silky texture, and a sweet, nutty taste. One bite and you'll find yourself truly enchanted.

FILE UNDER

Scales

QUANTITY	INGREDIENT
1 cup	forbidden rice
1	cinnamon stick
½ teaspoon	kosher salt
2 cups	unsweetened almond milk or coconut milk
¼ cup	pure maple syrup
1 teaspoon	vanilla extract

DIRECTIONS

1 Place the rice, cinnamon stick, and salt in a medium saucepan. Add 3 cups of water and bring to a boil over high heat, then reduce to a gentle simmer. Cover with a tight-fitting lid and cook until the rice is tender and all the liquid has been absorbed, 40 to 45 minutes. Remove and discard the cinnamon stick.

2 Stir in the milk, maple syrup, and vanilla. Increase the heat to high to bring back to a boil, then reduce to a simmer and cook, stirring occasionally, until thick and creamy, 35 to 40 minutes. Rice pudding can be served warm or chilled. If serving chilled, cover and chill for at least 4 hours before serving.

COOK'S NOTE: Although forbidden rice is sometimes called black rice (called so due to the color of the uncooked grains), it typically cooks up to a striking purple color, making this rice pudding particularly beautiful.

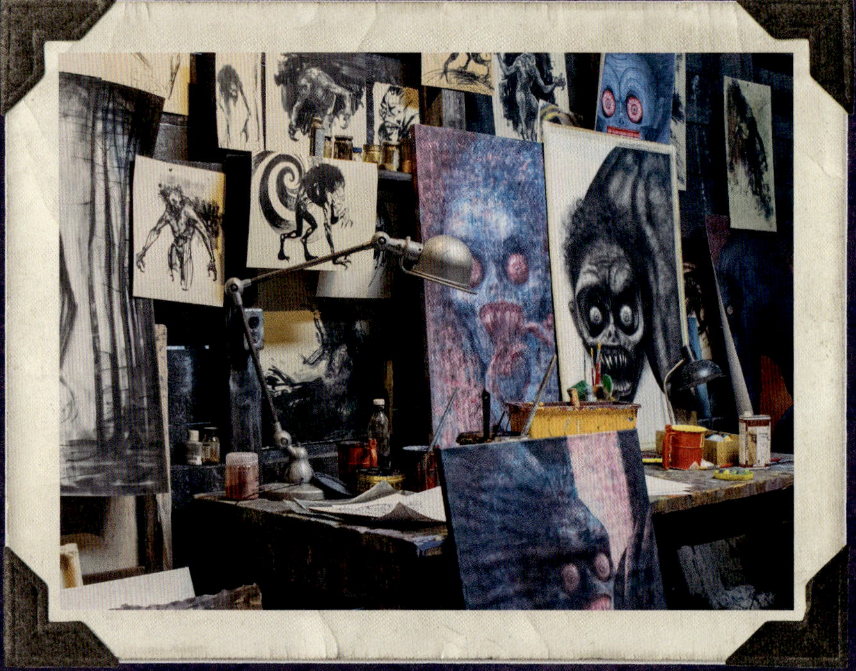

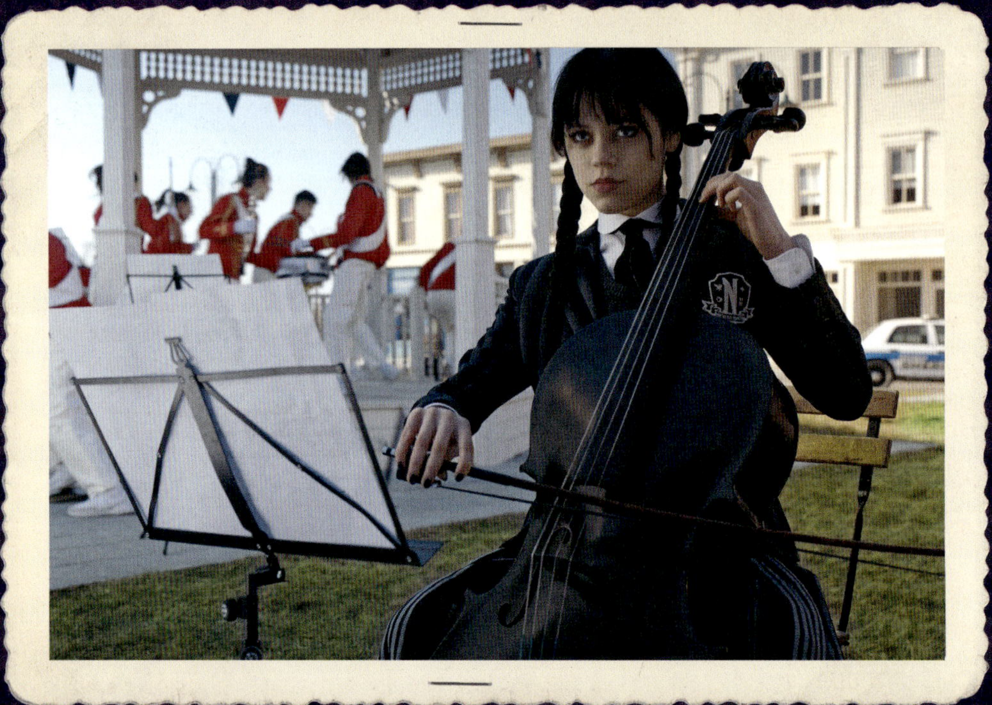

Buzzworthy Biscuits

✦◆✦◇✦

YIELD 2 DOZEN COOKIES   TIME 90 MINUTES PREP, 30 MINUTES BAKING

Sure, everyone loves a good sugar cookie. But you don't need psychic powers to divine that pure sweetness comes straight from the hive. Every day my fuzzy, buzzy babies work their bee-est to help their colony make honey that's as sweet as my dear friend Wednesday. (Mess with either and you'll get stung!) I use this honey to make my mothers' favorite recipe, a chewy, honey-sweetened cookie that would surely become the buzz around Nevermore Academy, if anyone besides Wednesday knew that I (or the cookies) even existed. But trust me: They're the bee's knees.

QUANTITY	INGREDIENT
2⅓ cups	all-purpose flour
1½ teaspoons	baking soda
12 tablespoons (1½ sticks)	unsalted butter, softened
½ cup	dark amber honey
½ cup	granulated sugar
1 teaspoon	ground cinnamon
	Pinch of ground cloves
	Pinch of nutmeg
1	large egg, room temperature
1 tablespoon	vanilla extract
¼ teaspoon	orange blossom water
¼ cup	raw sugar

DIRECTIONS

1 Whisk together the flour and baking soda in a medium bowl. Set aside.

2 Place the butter, honey, granulated sugar, cinnamon, cloves, and nutmeg in the bowl of a stand mixer fitted with a paddle attachment. Beat on medium-high speed until lightened in color and fluffy, 5 to 7 minutes. Scrape down the paddle and sides and bottom of the bowl about halfway through mixing and again at the end.

3 Add the egg, vanilla, and orange blossom water and mix until smooth, 2 to 4 minutes. Reduce the mixer speed to low and add the flour mixture. Mix until a soft, slightly sticky dough forms and no dry flour remains, 2 to 4 minutes.

4 Cover the bowl tightly with plastic wrap and chill for 1 hour. You may also chill overnight—if chilling for any longer than 1 hour, remove the dough from the bowl, shape into a disc, and wrap tightly with plastic wrap.

5 Heat the oven to 350°F. Line a half-sheet pan with parchment paper.

6 Place the raw sugar in a small bowl. Use a 2-tablespoon cookie scoop to portion out the dough. Roll each portion of dough into a ball, then roll the balls in the raw sugar.

7 Place 12 balls of dough on the prepared sheet pan, spacing them about 2 inches apart. Reserve the remaining balls of dough covered in the fridge. Bake until golden brown at the edges and the centers are just set, 12 to 14 minutes. Let cool on the pan for 5 minutes before transferring to a wire rack to cool completely before serving. Repeat the process with the remaining dough.

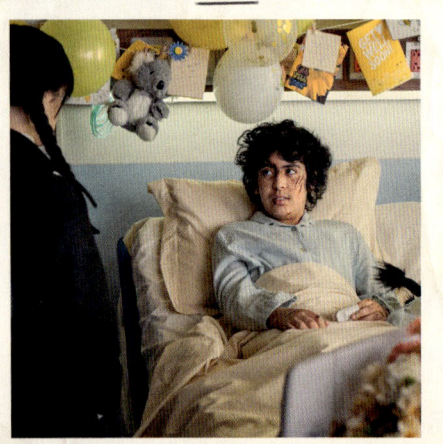

Thing's Pumpkin Pinkies

✦◦✦

YIELD 2 TO 3 POUNDS | **TIME** 20 MINUTES PREP, 90 MINUTES COOKING

People often ask me, Does Thing eat? And, truthfully, it is one of the Addams Family's last great mysteries. But I like to think that he prefers finger foods. And since Día de Muertos is about honoring family, I like to whip up a batch of calabaza en tacha—Mexican candied pumpkin—in his honor. It's a traditional Day of the Dead offering made of pumpkin slices that I cut into the shape of fingers, then simmer slowly in a mixture of cinnamon, cloves, and orange peel until they're soft and tender. Drizzle the digits in their own sauce and serve with whipped cream for a delicious dessert that will have you licking your fingers every time.

QUANTITY	INGREDIENT
1	medium sugar pumpkin, butternut squash, or kabocha squash (2 to 3 pounds)
1½ pounds	piloncillo or dark brown sugar
3	cinnamon sticks
2	whole cloves
2 tablespoons	orange zest
¼ cup	orange juice
½ teaspoon	kosher salt
1 cup	heavy cream
2 tablespoons	powdered sugar
	Ground cinnamon, to serve

DIRECTIONS

1 Rinse and scrub the pumpkin, then remove the stem and cut the pumpkin in half lengthwise. Use a spoon to scoop out and discard the seeds and fibers. Cut the pumpkin into long finger-like spears, 2 × 3 to 2 × 4 inches.

2 Place the piloncillo, cinnamon sticks, cloves, orange zest, orange juice, and salt in a large lidded saucepan or Dutch oven. Add 3 cups of water and stir over low heat until the sugar is dissolved. Add the pumpkin. Bring to a simmer and cover. Cook for 30 minutes, then gently scoop and toss the pumpkin pieces to rearrange them so that the bottom pieces are on top. Cover and cook until the pumpkin is tender and easily pierced by a fork, 20 to 30 minutes longer.

3 Carefully transfer the pumpkin to a serving dish. Cover it with foil and keep in a warm place. Increase the heat under the saucepan to bring the syrup to a boil. Cook, stirring occasionally, until reduced and thickened enough to coat the back of a spoon, 10 to 15 minutes (the time will vary depending on how much moisture the pumpkin gave off during simmering—rely on the visual cues here). Pour the syrup over the pumpkin.

4 Beat together the heavy cream and powdered sugar in a medium bowl with a handheld mixer until thickened but still a pourable consistency, 3 to 4 minutes. Serve the pumpkin with the sweetened cream and some ground cinnamon. Store leftover pumpkin in an airtight container in the fridge for up to 5 days.

Uncle Fester's Scout's Honor Cookies

+◊+

YIELD ABOUT **2** DOZEN COOKIES | TIME **90** MINUTES PREP, **30** MINUTES BAKING

FILED
Uncle Fester

While I never attended Nevermore Academy myself, I used to visit Gomez—usually with a dagger between my teeth and a fresh batch of his favorite Scout's Honor Cookies in my bag. On one visit a nosy Fur snuffed out my secret ingredient and reported me to the authorities, and suddenly I'm on vacay at the Zurich Institute for the Criminally Insane, in line for my very first lobotomy. But while my frontal lobe didn't entirely survive, this delightful recipe did! Chock-full of shredded coconut, chewy caramel, and chocolate drizzle, this version is almost as good as the original and less likely to send you to prison.

QUANTITY	INGREDIENT
	COOKIE BASE
8 tablespoons (1 stick)	unsalted butter, softened
¼ cup	granulated sugar
2 tablespoons	powdered sugar
¼ teaspoon	kosher salt
1	large egg white
1½ teaspoons	vanilla extract
1 cup	all-purpose flour, plus more for the work surface
2 tablespoons	cornstarch
	ASSEMBLY
½ cup	unsweetened shredded coconut
8 ounces	soft caramel candies, unwrapped
3 tablespoons	heavy cream
1 cup	semisweet or bittersweet chocolate

DIRECTIONS

1 *Make the cookie base:* Place the butter, both sugars, and salt in the bowl of a stand mixer fitted with a paddle attachment. Mix on medium-low speed, just until smooth and creamy, 2 to 4 minutes. With the mixer still running, add the egg white and vanilla. Mix until fully incorporated, about 2 minutes longer.

2 Reduce the mixer speed to low, then add the flour and cornstarch all at once. Mix until just incorporated and no dry flour remains, 2 to 3 minutes, scraping down the paddle and sides and bottom of the bowl with a rubber spatula about halfway through.

3 Divide the dough into two equal-size discs. Wrap each in plastic wrap and chill for at least 1 hour.

4 Heat the oven to 325°F. Line a half-sheet pan with parchment paper.

5 Transfer 1 disc of dough to a lightly floured work surface. Roll out the dough to a thickness of about ⅛ inch. Use a 2-inch round cookie cutter (or jar or glass) to cut out as many rounds as you can. Then use a ½-inch round cookie cutter (or a ½-inch round piping tip) to remove a ½-inch round from the center of each of the 2-inch cookies. Transfer the cookies to the prepared sheet pan, leaving 1 inch of space between each one. The ½-inch rounds can be gathered up with the remaining dough scraps.

QUANTITY	INGREDIENT (CONT.)	DIRECTIONS (CONT.)

6 Bake the cookies for 15 minutes until set and just beginning to turn golden brown at the edges. Let cool on the pan for 5 minutes, then transfer to a wire rack to cool completely. Repeat the process with the remaining dough. (The parchment paper can be saved and reused in step 12.)

7 *Assemble the cookies:* Once the cookies are cooled, tip the shredded coconut onto a clean half-sheet pan. Spread into an even layer and bake for 10 to 15 minutes, stirring every 3 to 5 minutes, until uniformly golden brown. Set aside.

8 Place the caramels and heavy cream in a medium saucepan and set over medium-low heat. Cook, stirring constantly with a rubber spatula, until fully melted and smooth. Transfer three-quarters of the melted caramel to a heatproof bowl. Set the remaining caramel aside.

9 Fold the toasted coconut into the larger portion of caramel. Set aside.

10 Spread a thin layer of plain caramel on the tops of each of the cookies, then spread 1 tablespoon of the coconut caramel mixture on top. Allow the caramel to set.

11 While the caramel sets, add the chocolate to a medium bowl set over a small pot of simmering water (be sure the bottom of the bowl isn't touching the water). Heat, stirring constantly, until melted and smooth.

12 Line two half-sheet pans with parchment paper. Dip the bottoms of each cookie into the melted chocolate, then transfer to the prepared sheet pans. Place the remaining chocolate in a piping bag. Snip the very tip off the piping bag, then drizzle the cookies with lines of chocolate. Allow the chocolate to set at room temperature before serving.

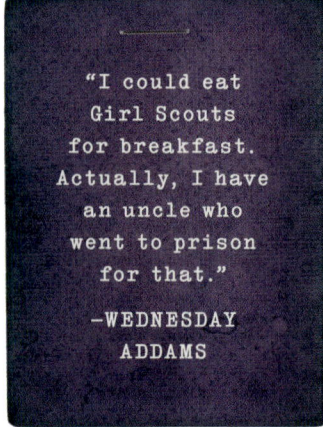
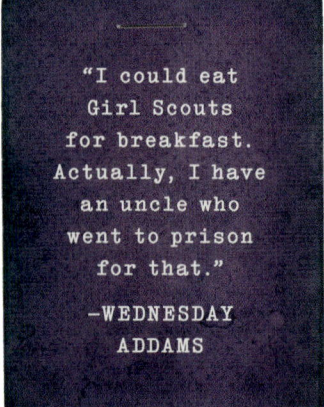

"I could eat
Girl Scouts
for breakfast.
Actually, I have
an uncle who
went to prison
for that."

—WEDNESDAY
ADDAMS

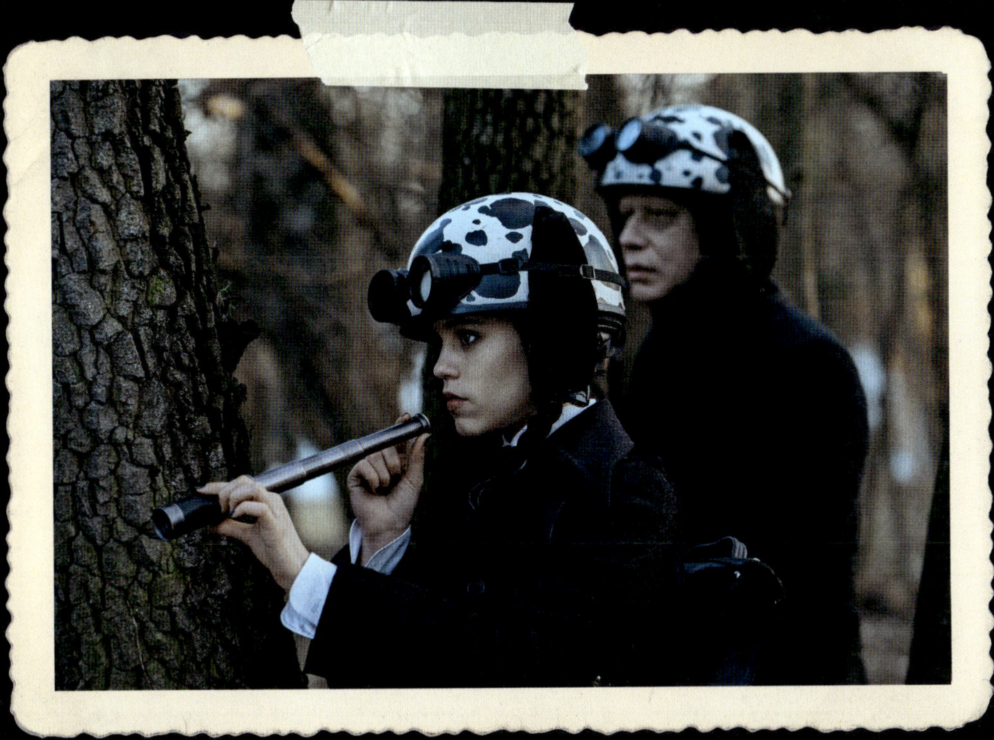
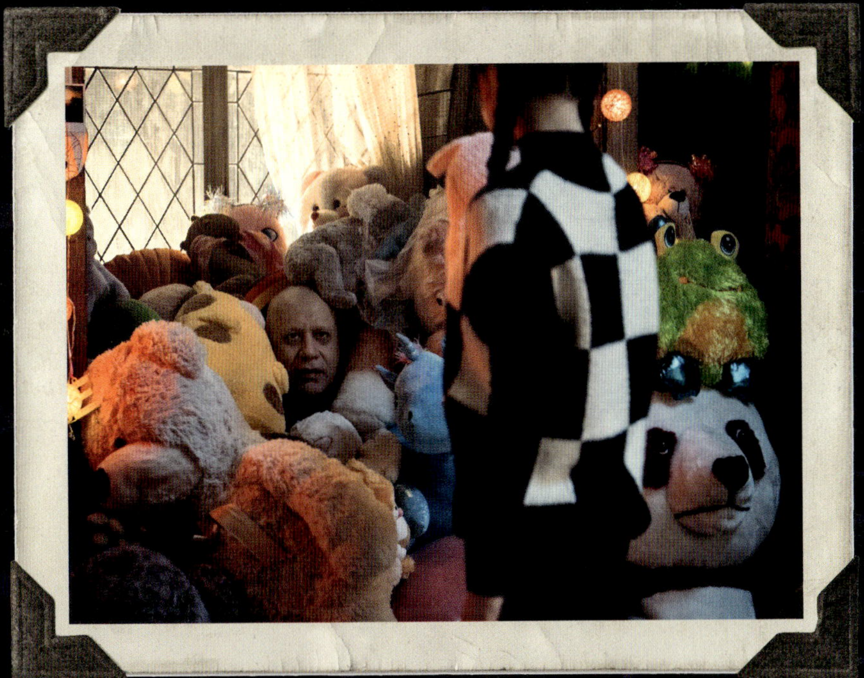

Nightshade Society Poe Parfait

✦◦✦○✦○✦○✦○✦○✦○✦○✦○✦○✦○✦○✦○✦○✦○✦○✦○✦◦✦

YIELD　　SERVES **4**　　　TIME **60** MINUTES PREP, **4** HOURS CHILLING, **20** MINUTES COOKING

The Nightshade Society is proud of its legacy and exceptionally selective of its membership. We can't just let any dorky denizen through our Edgar Allan Poe-guarded door. Luckily you won't need to solve the riddles or even know the secret snaps to partake in our signature parfait, named after our illustrious alumnus. Evoking the colors of the Nevermore Academy uniforms, this dessert has layers of ube custard, black cocoa sesame crumble, and ube whipped cream. It's so good, you won't be able to keep it a secret from society for long.

QUANTITY	INGREDIENT
	CRÈME PÂTISSIÈRE
3 tablespoons	cornstarch
⅔ cup	sugar
¼ teaspoon	kosher salt
4	large egg yolks
1½ cups	whole milk
½ cup	heavy cream
2 tablespoons	unsalted butter, cubed
½ teaspoon	ube extract
½ teaspoon	vanilla extract
	CRUMBLE
½ cup	all-purpose flour
¼ cup	lightly packed dark brown sugar
2 tablespoons	black cocoa powder
¼ cup	black sesame seeds
¼ teaspoon	kosher salt
1½ teaspoons	black sesame paste
4 tablespoons (½ stick)	cold unsalted butter, cubed

DIRECTIONS

1 *Make the crème pâtissière:* Whisk together the cornstarch, granulated sugar, and salt in a medium saucier or saucepan (a saucier works well here—the rounded bottom makes whisking easier). Whisk in the yolks, milk, and heavy cream until smooth.

2 Cook over medium heat, whisking constantly, until the mixture is thickened and begins to bubble, 8 to 10 minutes. At the 8-minute mark, stop whisking and watch for bubbling—the moment you see the first bubble, set a timer for 1 minute and whisk constantly. Once the timer goes off, remove from the heat.

3 Place the butter in a medium bowl. Pour the still-hot crème pâtissière through a fine-mesh strainer into the bowl with the butter, using a rubber spatula to help push it through. Discard any solids.

4 Whisk the ube extract and vanilla into the crème pâtissière. Cover with plastic wrap, pressing the plastic onto the surface of the crème pâtissière. Let cool slightly, then transfer to the fridge to chill for at least 4 hours.

5 *Make the crumble:* Heat the oven to 350°F. Line a half-sheet pan with parchment paper.

6 Whisk together the flour, brown sugar, cocoa powder, sesame seeds, and salt in a large bowl. Stir in the black sesame paste and butter with a fork. Work the mixture with your hands, rubbing the butter into the dry mixture until lentil- to pea-size clumps form.

QUANTITY	INGREDIENT (CONT.)
	WHIPPED CREAM
½ cup	heavy cream
2 tablespoons	powdered sugar
2 to 3 drops	ube extract
	Black sesame seeds, to garnish

DIRECTIONS (CONT.)

7 Scatter the crumble mixture over the prepared sheet pan. Bake for 10 minutes, gently toss with a heatproof spatula, then bake for 10 minutes longer until slightly darkened and dry. Transfer the sheet pan to a wire rack and allow to cool to room temperature.

8 *Make the whipped cream:* Place the heavy cream, powdered sugar, and ube extract in a large bowl. Beat with a handheld mixer, starting on low until the sugar is moistened, then increasing the speed to high until the mixture is thick and maintains soft peaks.

9 Remove the crème pâtissière from the fridge and whisk until smooth. Fill four 8-ounce clear dessert glasses with alternating layers of crème pâtissière and crumble until the glasses are full. Top with a dollop of ube whipped cream and a sprinkling of black sesame seeds.

COOK'S NOTE: The crumble and crème pâtissière can both be made up to 3 days in advance. Store the crème pâtissière in an airtight container in the fridge, and store the crumble in an airtight container at room temperature until you're ready to assemble. The whipped cream is best made the day of.

SHERIFF'S DEPT.
JERICHO, VERMONT

ADDAMS,GOMEZ

AG- 3436U2588

10.22.1

As Jericho as Apple Pie

✦•◦•✦•◦•✦•◦•✦•◦•✦•◦•✦•◦•✦•◦•✦•◦•✦•◦•✦•◦•✦•◦•✦•◦•✦•◦•✦•◦•✦•◦•✦

YIELD ONE 9-INCH DEEP-DISH PIE | TIME 90 MINUTES PREP, 60 MINUTES BAKING

Nevermore Academy may have its share of creepy cakes and cookies, but here at Pilgrim World we pride ourselves on pie. And we're delighted to have this particular pie, known as the Marlborough, included in this cookbook as a substitution for our fudge recipe, which was not deemed authentic by whatever fiend at Nevermore Academy is vetting these things. (Sorry, still a bit bitter.) This traditional pie once elegantly graced many a colonial table each Thanksgiving. Unlike its more well-known cousin, the boring old apple pie, the Marlborough pie boasts an apple-infused custard on top of a flaky crust. Just one bite and you'll be transported back to the good old days of Pilgrims and progress.

FILED
Pilgrim world

QUANTITY	INGREDIENT	DIRECTIONS
	CRUST	**1** *Make the crust:* Place the flour, granulated sugar, salt, and butter in the bowl of a food processor. Pulse to combine, until the mixture resembles wet sand, about 2 minutes.
1½ cups	all-purpose flour, plus more for the work surface	
1 tablespoon	granulated sugar	**2** Transfer the contents of the food processor to a large bowl. Add the cold water and stir until a shaggy dough forms. Knead the dough with your hands until relatively smooth, about 2 minutes. Shape the dough into a disc, wrap with plastic wrap, and chill for 1 hour.
¾ teaspoon	kosher salt	
8 tablespoons (1 stick)	unsalted butter, cut into ½-inch cubes	
3 tablespoons	cold water	
	FILLING	**3** *While the dough chills, make the filling:* Place the apples, apple cider, and sherry in a medium saucepan. Cook over medium heat, stirring occasionally, until the apples break down into a thick, chunky sauce, 15 to 20 minutes. Remove from the heat, stir in the brown sugar, butter, cinnamon, cloves, nutmeg, and salt, then allow to cool. Add lemon juice.
4	Granny Smith apples, peeled, cored, and diced	
½ cup	apple cider	
½ cup	dry sherry or additional apple cider (see Cook's Note)	
¾ cup	lightly packed light brown sugar	**4** Beat together the eggs and heavy cream in a medium bowl until combined. Whisk in the apple mixture and set aside.
4 tablespoons (½ stick)	unsalted butter	**5** Place an oven rack in the lower third position of the oven. Heat the oven to 350°F.
1 teaspoon	ground cinnamon	
¼ teaspoon	ground cloves	**6** Place the chilled dough on a lightly floured surface. Roll out to a thickness of ¼ inch. Carefully transfer to a pie plate. Trim the dough to create a ½-inch overhang, then crimp the edges as you like, either with a fork or by pinching for a more decorative edge.
	Pinch of freshly grated nutmeg	
¼ teaspoon	kosher salt	
2 tablespoons	lemon juice	

QUANTITY	INGREDIENT (CONT.)	DIRECTIONS (CONT.)
4	eggs	
1 cup	heavy cream	
	Whipped cream, to serve	

7 Pour the filling into the prepared crust, then set the pie plate onto a half-sheet pan. Bake for 50 to 60 minutes, until golden brown and the center of the pie has a slight wobble. Transfer the pie plate to a wire rack and allow to cool to room temperature. Serve at room temperature or chilled, with homemade or store-bought whipped cream. Tightly cover leftover pie with plastic wrap or foil and store in the fridge for up to 3 days.

COOK'S NOTE: Sherry will impart the most traditional taste and give this pie a unique flavor, but if you're avoiding alcohol, you can replace it with additional apple cider.

GREETINGS FROM PILGRIM WORLD

Goody's Ghost

❖◦○◦❖◦○◦❖◦○◦❖◦○◦❖◦○◦❖◦○◦❖◦○◦❖◦○◦❖◦○◦❖◦○◦❖◦○◦❖

YIELD **10** TO **15** GHOSTS TIME **15** MINUTES PREP, **90** MINUTES BAKING, **90** MINUTES RESTING

My ancestor Goody Addams didn't have an easy life. Labeled a witch, a sorceress, and Lucifer's mistress—and those were just the compliments!—she was almost murdered by Joseph Crackstone in 1692, after trying to stick up for Outcasts. Recently, she came back from the dead as a ghost to help destroy Crackstone all over again. I admire her tenacity—and the fact that she agreed to assist me with my psychic abilities. I found the recipe for these piped, ghost-shaped meringues in the secret library, and they are as quirky and creepy as their namesake. And if you're lucky, maybe they'll entice a helpful spirit to reside in you too.

QUANTITY	INGREDIENT	DIRECTIONS
2	large egg whites	**1** Heat the oven to 200°F. Line a half-sheet pan with parchment paper and set aside.
	Pinch of cream of tartar	
	Pinch of kosher salt	**2** Place the egg whites, cream of tartar, and salt in the bowl of a stand mixer fitted with a whisk attachment. Beat on medium speed until thickened and frothy, then increase the speed to medium-high. Add the sugar a little bit at a time and continue mixing until glossy, stiff peaks form, 5 to 8 minutes, depending on the strength of your mixer. Add the vanilla and beat to incorporate, about 1 minute longer. Transfer the meringue to a large piping bag fitted with a large round piping tip. (Alternatively, you can use a gallon-size ziplock bag with a ¾-inch hole snipped off from one of the corners.)
⅓ cup	sugar	
¼ teaspoon	vanilla extract, preferably clear	
4 ounces	dark chocolate	

3 Pipe round, swirly little mounds 2 to 3 inches tall on the prepared sheet pan, leaving at least 1 inch between each ghost. Bake for 80 to 90 minutes, until the meringues look dry and are crisp to the touch. Turn off the heat and leave the meringues in the oven with the door closed until the oven is room temperature, 1 to 1½ hours longer.

4 Place the chocolate in a small microwave-safe bowl. Heat for 30 seconds on high and stir. Repeat the process until the chocolate is completely melted and smooth. Let cool slightly.

5 Dip the bottoms of each ghost in the chocolate, then return them to the sheet pan. Use a toothpick or very fine cake decorating brush to paint eyes and mouths on each of the ghosts. Let the chocolate set at room temperature. Eat as is or use to decorate the Rave to the Grave Cake (page 145).

6

SINISTER SIPS

There's a saying among vampires: "A night without blood is like a night without moonshine." While we can't personally vouch for that, we do know that the right mocktail can really punch up a party. For every Rave'N Ball, we create a unique signature drink to match the year's theme. Last year we invented the famous Yetitini (page 200), a sparkling blue mocktail designed for our latest ball, themed Climate Crisis Meets Extinction Event. Then there's the Make It Black! (page 176) blackberry mocktail made with luster dust that perfectly captured the mood at the Goth and Glamour event back in 1990 and is now the preferred drink of our new student Wednesday Addams.

Mocktails are mixed up on less formal occasions as well, often by students rumored to be members of the officially disbanded Nightshade Society. While we certainly don't know anything about any illegal clubs on campus, student Yoko Tanaka has been known to make a killer virgin mojito. While Yoko insists she'll give away her secret recipe only on her deathbed (which could be several centuries away, considering vampire longevity), she was willing to share the society's former signature drink, the Nightshade Society Nightcap (page 191).

Mocktails are just the beginning of our offerings. We also have coffee drink recipes for those who like their creepiness caffeinated. You'll find a quick Stone Cold Brew (page 184), ready to rock the world of any Stoner who wakes up too sleepy for school. And we've even allowed the Weathervane to submit its Daily Matcha Latte (page 197), once favored by a certain Nevermore Academy botany teacher in red boots. She may no longer be with us, but her drink of choice remains on the menu and now you can re-create it at home every time the Weathervane's espresso machine is broken.

If life's giving you lemons, try one of these sinister sips to darken up your day. Whether you prefer your drink black or bubbly, bloody or bright as a rainbow, or just extra caffeinated for a jolt before gym class, we have a Nevermore Academy-inspired sip for you.

Note: The drinks listed in this book are all alcohol-free, seeing as our students are under the legal age. However, if you are old enough to imbibe, feel free to add your own mix-ins to any of the recipes to give them a little extra bite.

Make It Black!

YIELD 1 MOCKTAIL   **TIME** 20 MINUTES

I don't know who designs the drinks at Nevermore Academy, but whoever it is should seriously have their license taken away. The obnoxious blue color of that monstrosity they call the Yetitini (page 200) was enough to make me break out in hives. If I'm making a mocktail, you better believe it'll be as murky as a black hole at the end of the universe where stars go to die. Think: Abandon all hope, all ye who drink here. Of course it's not easy to get the right color without mixing in a little black tar like Uncle Fester has been known to do. But I have found that black luster dust mixed with blackberry syrup can give the same effect, and unlike tar, it won't literally poison you.

QUANTITY	INGREDIENT	DIRECTIONS
	SIMPLE SYRUP	**1** *Make the simple syrup:* Place the blackberries, lime juice, and sugar in a small saucepan and add 1 cup of water. Bring to a boil over medium-high heat, then reduce to a simmer. Allow to simmer for 10 minutes, then pour the syrup through a fine-mesh strainer into a small bowl, using a rubber spatula to help push it through. Discard any solids. Let cool to room temperature.
2 cups	fresh or frozen blackberries	
2 tablespoons	lime juice	
1 cup	sugar	
	MOCKTAIL	**2** *Make the mocktail:* Fill a cocktail mixing glass or shaker with ice. Add 2 ounces of the blackberry simple syrup and the lime juice, then stir. Gently stir in the ginger beer and luster dust. Strain into a cocktail glass, garnish with the blackberries, and serve. Store leftover syrup in an airtight container in the fridge for up to 2 weeks.
½ ounce	lime juice	
8 ounces	ginger beer	
¼ teaspoon	black luster dust	
	Blackberries, to garnish	

COOK'S NOTE: Luster dust is a powdered pigment that gives a metallic shine to drinks and dishes. You may also use petal dust, which gives a matte finish and won't have the glittery, shimmery look, but will still help make the drink black. Both can be found easily online or at specialty baking supply shops and some craft stores.

> "I don't believe in heaven or hell. But I do believe in revenge. I usually serve it warm with a side of pain."
>
> —WEDNESDAY ADDAMS

Make It Pink!

+◊

YIELD **1** MOCKTAIL   TIME **40** MINUTES

I know you might think a blog isn't a big deal, but actually it's a huge responsibility and a bit of a time suck. Not that I mind, of course! I'm completely committed to keeping our community informed. But sometimes when writing I get seriously thirsty, and a glass of water is just way too boring and bland. So in cases like these, I like to make this *gorge* tea-infused mocktail that ends up being the most beautiful pink color you've ever seen and as sweet as my sweetie pie, Ajax. It's made from hibiscus iced tea, which is totally caffeine-free (so as not to keep you up on non-full moon nights) and is sweetened with muddled fresh raspberries and simple syrup. One sip and I promise you, you'll feel pretty in pink.

FILE UNDER

Enid

QUANTITY	INGREDIENT
	TEA
½ cup	dried hibiscus flowers
½	cinnamon stick
1 tablespoon	agave syrup
	SIMPLE SYRUP
2 cups	raspberries
2 tablespoons	lime juice
1 cup	sugar
	MOCKTAIL
½ ounce	lime juice
4 ounces	seltzer
¼ teaspoon	pink luster dust
	Raspberries, to garnish

DIRECTIONS

1 *Make the tea:* Bring 2 cups of water to a boil in a medium saucepan over high heat. Stir in the hibiscus and cinnamon stick. Cover, remove from heat, and let steep for 30 minutes. Strain out and discard the solids, then stir in the agave syrup while the tea is still hot. Let come to room temperature.

2 *Make the simple syrup:* Place the raspberries, lime juice, and sugar in a small saucepan and add 1 cup of water. Bring to a boil over medium-high heat, then reduce to a simmer. Allow to simmer for 10 minutes, then pour the syrup through a fine-mesh strainer into a small bowl, using a rubber spatula to help push it through. Discard the solids. Let cool to room temperature.

3 *Make the mocktail:* Fill a cocktail mixing glass or shaker with ice. Add 2 ounces of the raspberry simple syrup, the lime juice, and 4 ounces of the hibiscus tea, then stir. Gently stir in the seltzer and luster dust. Strain into a cocktail glass, garnish with the raspberries, and serve. Store leftover tea in an airtight container in the fridge for up to 1 week. Store leftover syrup in an airtight container in the fridge for up to 2 weeks.

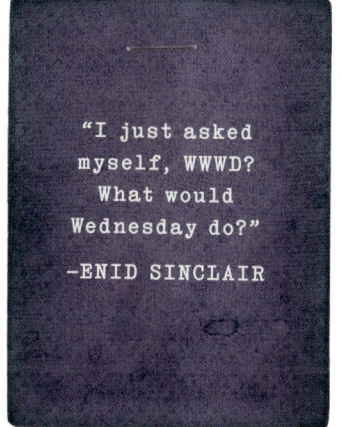

"I just asked myself, WWWD? What would Wednesday do?"

—ENID SINCLAIR

Bloody Mary

YIELD	1 MOCKTAIL	TIME	5 MINUTES

There are so many ridiculous myths surrounding Fangs. Like we can't go out in the daytime. Or we can turn into bats at will. If only. But the funniest myth is that we can't see our reflection in mirrors. How else would we do our hair in the morning? In fact, some Fangs even play a mirror game called Bloody Mary, where they whisper the evil spirit's name three times in a mirror, inviting her to come hang out (she's actually quite nice once you get to know her, though she totally cheats at cards). Mary was the one to introduce us to this drink, which has become a Fang fave. She uses real blood, but here we modify it with a tomato base. It's spicy, salty, and fangfully fresh!

QUANTITY	INGREDIENT	DIRECTIONS
4 ounces	tomato juice	Fill a rocks glass with ice. Add the tomato juice, pickle brine, celery salt, pepper, Worcestershire sauce, and hot sauce. Stir well with a cocktail stirrer. Garnish with the celery and pickle, then serve.
½ ounce	pickle brine	
¼ teaspoon	celery salt	
	Big pinch of freshly ground black pepper	
2	dashes of Worcestershire sauce	
3	dashes of hot sauce	
1	celery stalk, to garnish	
1	pickle spear, to garnish	

Bee Refreshed

◆◇◆◇◆◇◆◇◆◇◆◇◆◇◆◇◆◇◆◇◆◇◆◇◆◇◆◇◆◇◆◇◆◇◆◇◆◇◆

YIELD	**8** CUPS	TIME	**20** MINUTES

FILE UNDER
Eugene

These days it's hard to find someone who respects the ancient art of beekeeping. And until Wednesday arrived, I was both president and the only member in good standing of the Beekeeping Club at Nevermore Academy. Fortunately, my hive is good company. And through their gift of honey, I've been able to experiment with some amazing recipes, like this lavender lemonade that uses a simple syrup made of honey rather than sugar and infused with dry lavender. I mean, buzzworthy, right? Mix it in with fresh lemon juice and you have a drink that's sweet and refreshing and will have you buzzing.

QUANTITY	INGREDIENT	DIRECTIONS
	SIMPLE SYRUP	**1** *Make the simple syrup:* Place the honey, sugar, lavender, and salt in a small saucepan and add 1 cup of water. Bring to a boil over medium-high heat, stirring until the sugar has dissolved. Remove from the heat, cover, and let steep for 15 minutes. Strain out and dispose of the lavender and let come to room temperature.
½ cup	honey	
½ cup	sugar	
1 tablespoon	culinary lavender buds	
¼ teaspoon	kosher salt	
1 cup	fresh lemon juice	**2** Pour the prepared syrup and lemon juice into a 3-quart pitcher and add 6 cups of water. Stir well. Serve over ice. You can also make the syrup in advance and store it an airtight container in the fridge for up to 2 weeks.

Stone Cold Brew

YIELD	6 CUPS COLD BREW CONCENTRATE	TIME	20 MINUTES PREP, 24 HOURS RESTING

Not gonna lie, it can be super hard for Stoners to motivate in the mornings. Waking up from that stone-cold slumber is just brutal, even on the best of days, and let's just say most snakes aren't morning reptiles. To help get us to class on time, we've created this spiced cold brew coffee that can be prepared the day before and drunk immediately upon waking. It's made with coffee and spices that are ground together and steeped in cold water for 24 hours. It tastes great and will give you that much-needed jolt to rock your morning.

FILE UNDER
Stoners

QUANTITY	INGREDIENT
4	cinnamon sticks, broken into pieces
3	cardamom pods
1 pound	coffee beans, coarsely ground
½ teaspoon	ground ginger
1	spent vanilla bean pod, or 1 teaspoon vanilla powder
8 cups	filtered water, plus more as needed
	Whole milk or plant-based milk, such as almond or oat (optional)

DIRECTIONS

1. Pulse the cinnamon sticks and cardamom pods in a spice grinder until very coarsely ground, 15 to 20 seconds. The spices should just be broken apart in large pieces.

2. Line a 4-quart pitcher with a cold brew filter bag. Add the ground coffee beans, the ground-up cinnamon and cardamom, the ginger, vanilla bean pod, and 4 cups of the filtered water. Stir with a spoon for 5 minutes. It will start to foam—this is carbon dioxide releasing from the ground coffee beans.

3. Add the remaining 4 cups filtered water, stir, then cover the pitcher with its lid or a small plate and let sit at room temperature for 24 hours. Lift up the filter bag, set a fine-mesh strainer over the pitcher, then set the bag in the strainer and allow it to drain for 10 minutes.

4. Carefully pour the concentrate into a large airtight container, being careful not to let any sediment flow into the new container. Discard the sediment (you will lose a bit of the concentrate here). Store the concentrate in the fridge for up to 2 weeks.

5. To use the concentrate, mix 2 parts concentrate to 3 parts cold filtered water or milk, if using.

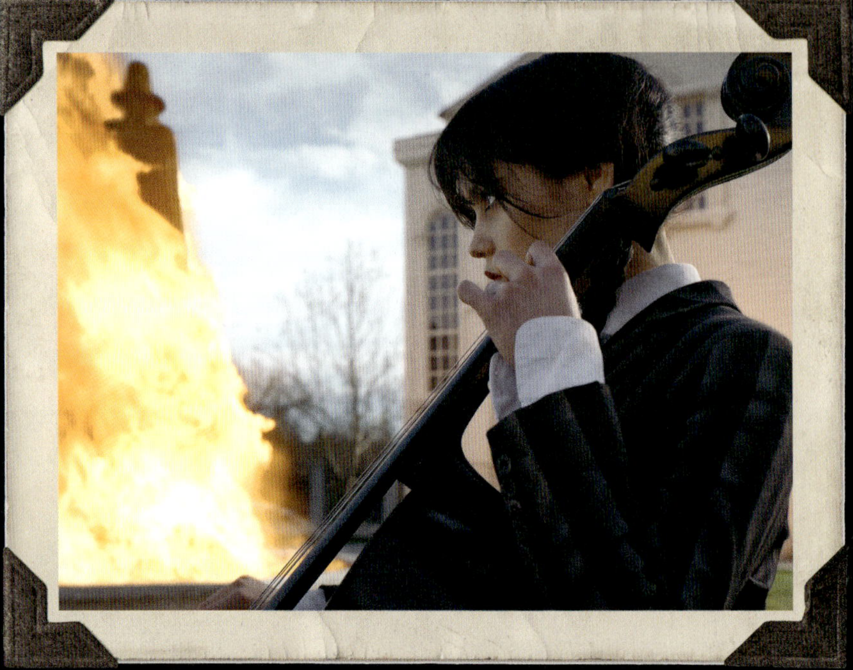

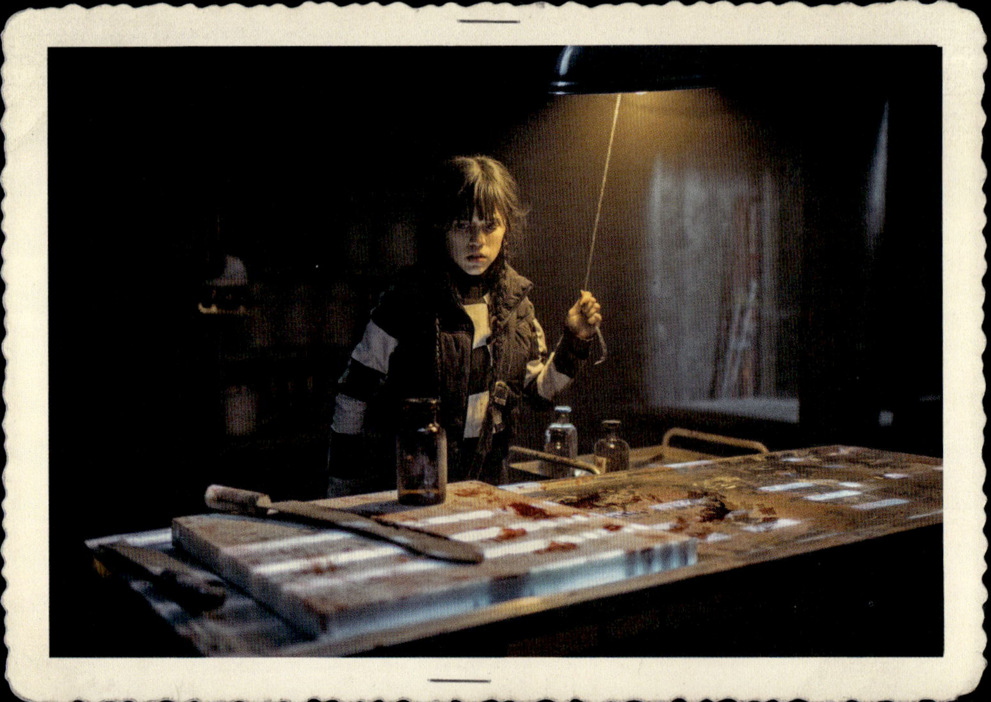

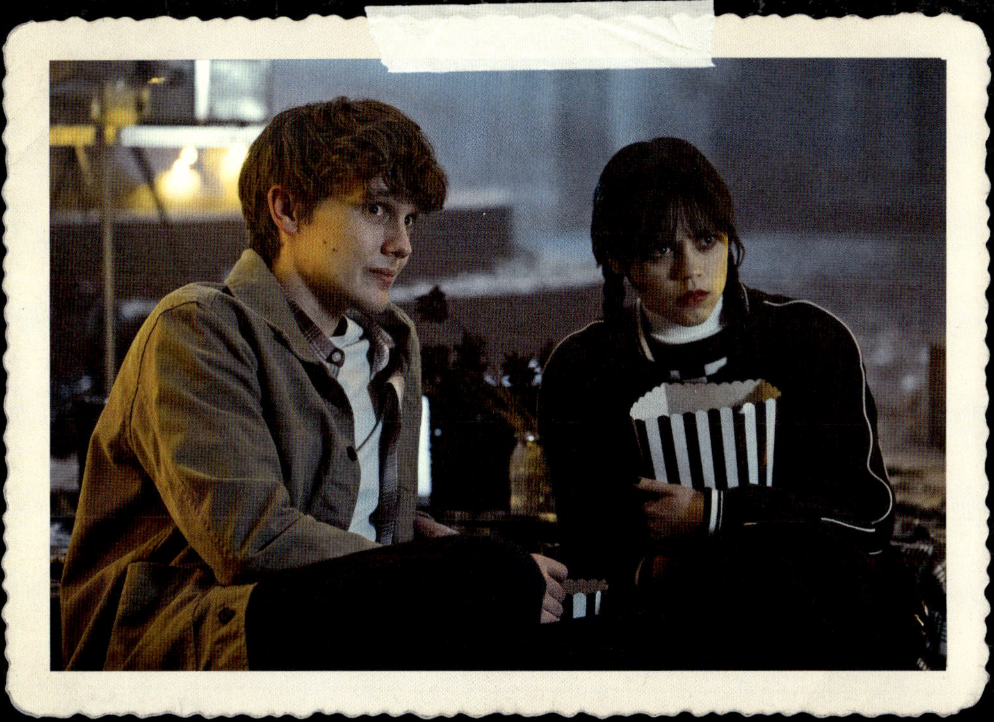

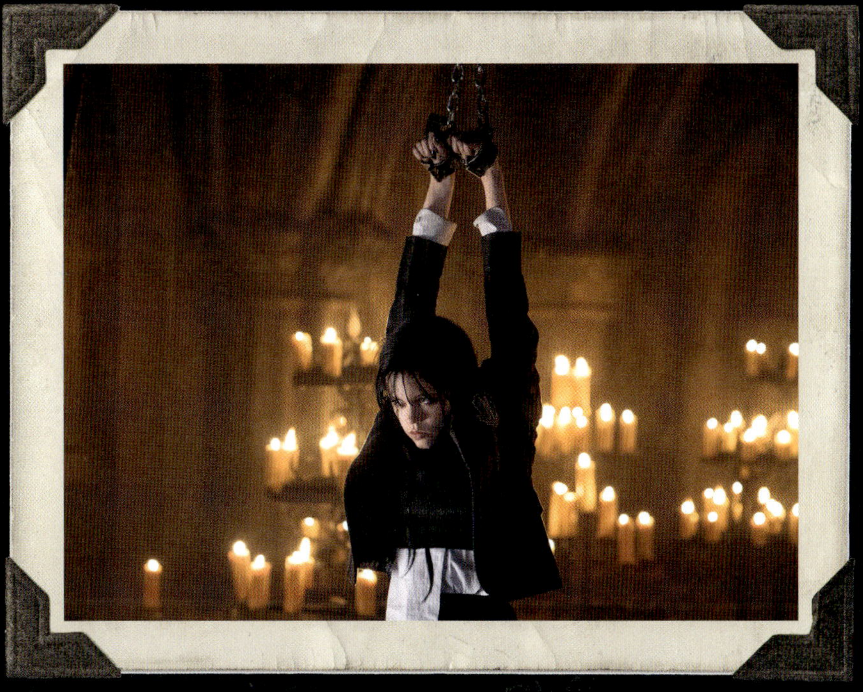

FILED
Morticia

Mija's Mud

✦◦✦

YIELD SERVES **4**	TIME **15** MINUTES

When Wednesday was just a little storm cloud, some nights she'd come down from her room, unable to sleep, her mind buzzing with life's most important questions, like *Is it better to kill or be killed?* or *Which career pays more: writer or contract killer?* To help her self-depress, I'd mix her up a cup of champurrado, a Mexican hot chocolate concoction. It's made with Mexican dark chocolate and cinnamon and thickened into a nice mud-like paste with the addition of masa harina (a type of corn flour). As good as drinking from an actual mud puddle but without the acid rain aftertaste.

QUANTITY	INGREDIENT
1 cup	warm water
½ cup	masa harina
3 cups	whole milk or plant-based milk, such as almond or oat
4 ounces	Mexican dark chocolate, coarsely chopped
¼ cup	lightly packed piloncillo or dark brown sugar
½ teaspoon	ground cinnamon, plus more to serve
¼ teaspoon	kosher salt

DIRECTIONS

1 Place the warm water in a medium saucier or saucepan (a saucier works well here—the rounded bottom makes whisking easier) over medium heat. Whisking constantly, add the masa harina a little bit at a time. Whisk until smooth and thick.

2 Whisk in the milk, then increase the heat to medium-high. Whisk in the chocolate, piloncillo, cinnamon, and salt. Continue whisking until the chocolate has melted and the mixture is smooth. Once the mixture begins to bubble, lower the heat to maintain a bare simmer—the mixture should bubble lazily here and there—and whisk constantly for 5 minutes.

3 Remove from the heat and give the mixture one last vigorous, continuous whisk for 30 seconds to create a nice thick froth on top. Divide among four mugs, sprinkle with more cinnamon, and let cool slightly before sipping. The masa mixture retains heat *very* well, so the drink will stay quite hot for a while.

SINISTER SIPS

Nightshade Society Nightcap

| YIELD | ABOUT 6 CUPS | TIME | 10 MINUTES PREP, 8 TO 12 HOURS CHILLING |

The Nightshade Society is a very elite social club, which means it needs a signature drink as sophisticated as its membership. As the society's official amateur mixologist, I take my role very seriously. So when crafting a signature cocktail for our club? I decided to base it on horchata (pronounced or-CHAT-ta), a sweet cinnamon rice drink popular in Mexico. My version has a special Nightshade Society twist. By replacing regular white rice with forbidden rice, which was once reserved only for the wealthy and powerful (just like our membership), the drink takes on a sophisticated violet hue.

QUANTITY	INGREDIENT
1 cup	forbidden rice
1 cup	blanched almonds
½ cup	sugar
2 teaspoons	ground cinnamon
½ teaspoon	kosher salt
2 cups	whole milk or plant-based milk, such as almond or oat
	Simple syrup, to serve (see Cook's Note)

DIRECTIONS

1 Blitz together the rice and almonds in the bowl of a food processor until finely ground. Pour this into a blender and add the sugar, cinnamon, salt, and 4 cups of water. Blend until smooth, 3 to 5 minutes.

2 Pour the contents of the blender into an airtight container and chill in the fridge overnight or up to 12 hours.

3 Line a fine-mesh strainer with two layers of cheesecloth and set the strainer over a large pitcher or bowl. Pour the horchata through the strainer, using a rubber spatula to push it through. Discard the solids. Whisk the milk into the horchata.

4 Fill a glass with ice. Add simple syrup to taste, then fill the glass with horchata. Stir and serve.

COOK'S NOTE: If you don't have simple syrup at the ready, you can make it by simmering 1 cup water with 1 cup sugar until the sugar is dissolved. Let it cool to room temperature before using. Store in an airtight container in the fridge for up to 2 weeks. Make it a dirty horchata by adding up to ¼ cup Stone Cold Brew (page 184) to an 8-ounce serving.

"The Nightshades are an elite social club. Emphasis on elite."

—BIANCA BARCLAY

WHAT IS THE
Nightshade Society?

If you haven't heard of us? It's probably for good reason, no offense. The Nightshade Society is the most elite of the elite clubs at Nevermore Academy. Founded by Goody Addams centuries ago to fight for Outcast rights, today we operate in a more *unofficial* capacity after we lost our charter thirty years ago due to an unfortunate incident with a normie. But the school principal does allow us to continue to meet secretly, thanks to the influence of our illustrious (and wealthy) alumni, including Morticia Addams, who once served as our fearless leader.

These days, the Nightshade Society tends to focus more on social events than on social justice, which, as you can imagine, is a lot more fun and has less chance of members getting murdered. We're talking exclusive rooftop parties, weekend campouts, and even the occasional skinny-dip. (We warn you: It can get pretty wild!) As a member, you'll also be eligible to purchase a limited-edition designer mask and purple hooded cloak to wear at our midnight meetings in the library so everyone will know you're part of the crew. Once you've been a member in good standing for a year, our current resident mixologist, Yoko Tanaka, will design a signature cocktail in your honor. Honestly, no one in their right mind would refuse an invitation (save for Wednesday Addams, but her state of mind has been greatly debated).

How does one score an invite to this secret society? *Here are a few pro tips:*

- **BE IMPRESSIVE.** Remember, we accept only the best of the best.

- **BE A LEGACY.** If you have a parent or an ancestor who was a member, you've got a leg up on the competition.

- **HAVE A CURRENT MEMBER** sponsor you. Our roster is secret, so you'll have to guess who to impress. That said, we still have to vote, so it's not a guarantee.

- **DON'T MAKE WAVES.** We can't have troublemakers threaten our underground status.

- **SOLVE THE RIDDLE** of the Poe statue. That'll get you through the door—literally—but it doesn't necessarily mean we'll accept you once inside.

If you can't manage any of these, I'm sorry, but perhaps this secret society is not your speed. May we suggest the Hummers instead? We hear they're just buzzing for new members!

Undersea Pearl Tea

Whether you're sunning yourself somewhere in the Seychelles or just psyching yourself up to fence with a psychic, this Scales' version of a boba tea is as alluring as any siren's song. By mixing up taro powder with green tea and milk, you'll achieve a pretty pearlescent-purple color, resembling the inside of a seashell. And while we fins traditionally top off our teas with caviar or roe, you can swap them out for tapioca boba pearls for a sweeter, less fishy taste. So good, it will have you singing after one sip.

FILE UNDER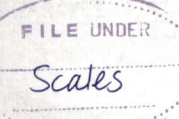
Scales

QUANTITY	INGREDIENT	DIRECTIONS
	SIMPLE SYRUP	**1** *Make the simple syrup:* Place the brown sugar in a small saucepan, add ½ cup of water, and bring to a boil. Let cool to room temperature, then chill in an airtight container in the fridge for 4 hours. This can be made up to 2 weeks in advance.
½ cup	lightly packed light brown sugar	
	BOBA TEA	**2** *Make the tea:* Mix together the tapioca pearls and the chilled brown sugar syrup in a small bowl. Set aside to soak for 15 minutes.
½ cup	black tapioca pearls, cooked and cooled	
¼ cup	unsweetened taro powder	**3** Place the taro powder, jasmine tea, milk, ube extract, and luster dust in a blender and add 1 cup of ice. Blend on low speed, gradually increasing to high speed, until smooth, about 1 minute.
1 cup	jasmine green tea, chilled	
1 cup	whole milk or plant-based milk, such as almond or oat	
3 drops	ube extract	**4** Use a slotted spoon to divide the tapioca pearls between two 16-ounce glasses, leaving the majority of the brown sugar syrup behind in the bowl. Top with ice, then divide the milk tea between both glasses. Sweeten to taste with the remaining brown sugar syrup.
½ teaspoon	pearl luster dust	

FOUNDED IN 1791

NEVERMORE ACADEMY

UNITAS EST INVICTA

Daily Matcha Latte

YIELD **1** LATTE   TIME **5** MINUTES

On days our espresso maker isn't broken, you can rely on our resident baristas to whip up pretty much any drink under the sun (or moon) at the Weathervane, and we're delighted to be asked to contribute to this cookbook. Our regulars can be pretty predictable, so we usually know their orders, if not their names. Case in point: a certain normie teacher in red boots who ordered the matcha latte so often that we changed the drink's name in her honor (then abruptly changed it back again once we learned her true nature). In any case, the Daily Matcha Latte may not be creepy, but it is creamy and delicious. And once you learn how to make it, maybe you can apply for a job here? We do have an opening . . .

QUANTITY	INGREDIENT	DIRECTIONS
1¼ teaspoons	ceremonial grade matcha powder	**1** Sift the matcha powder into a 12-ounce mug. Add the hot water and whisk until smooth. Whisk in the maple syrup.
1 tablespoon	hot water	
1 teaspoon	pure maple syrup, plus more to taste	**2** Use a milk frother to froth the milk until doubled in volume. Pour the frothed milk into the mug in a swirling motion, topping with the foam. Sweeten to taste with additional maple syrup, if desired.
¾ cup	hot whole milk or plant-based milk, such as almond or oat (see Cook's Note)	

COOK'S NOTE: You could also start with cold milk and froth it using a steamer.

"Drip is for people who hate themselves and know their lives have no purpose or meaning."

—WEDNESDAY ADDAMS

Dry Ice Delights

Most normies don't realize that dry ice
for drinks is relatively simple to obtain and
safe to use as long as it's not swallowed.
While we at Nevermore Academy keep a freezer full
of the stuff for regular everyday use, it can
also be acquired at many normie grocery stores
and costs one to three dollars a pound.

ALWAYS USE GLOVES OR TONGS
(never your bare hands!) to drop the dry ice
into your already-filled punch bowl. The pellets
will sink to the bottom of the bowl, and the
smoky effect will begin instantly as the dry ice
begins to melt, lasting about 5 minutes. Spoon
the punch into cups and serve the smoky drinks
to your partygoers, leaving the dry ice itself in
the punch bowl until it completely dissolves.

FUN FACT: It's a common misconception
that dry ice contains liquid nitrogen. It's
actually made from frozen carbon dioxide.

Yetitini

◆•◇•◆•◇•◆•◇•◆•◇•◆•◇•◆•◇•◆•◇•◆•◇•◆•◇•◆•◇•◆•◇•◆•◇•◆•◇•◆•◇•◆•◇•◆•◇•◆•◇•◆

| YIELD | 2 MOCKTAILS | TIME | 20 MINUTES PREP, 10 MINUTES COOLING |

When your event's theme is Extinction, you can't just serve something as simple as soda. Introducing the Yetitini, an icy, refreshing libation inspired by the now tragically extinct Yetis. (Note: Please don't refer to Yetis as Abominable Snowmen—that term is considered offensive.) If you serve this sparkling mocktail in a punch bowl with dry ice, it leaves a smoky trail. It's sweet, it's sparkly, and it's guaranteed to leave you chilled!

QUANTITY	INGREDIENT
	SIMPLE SYRUP
1 cup	diced cucumber
1 cup	fresh mint leaves
1 cup	sugar
	MOCKTAIL
½ ounce	lemon juice
½ ounce	lime juice
12 ounces	seltzer or sparkling water
¼ teaspoon	metallic blue luster dust

DIRECTIONS

1 *Make the simple syrup:* Place the cucumber, mint leaves, and sugar in a small saucepan and add 1 cup of water. Bring to a boil over medium-high heat, then reduce to a simmer. Allow to simmer for 10 minutes, then pour the syrup through a fine-mesh strainer into a small bowl, using a rubber spatula to help push it through. Discard the solids. Let cool to room temperature.

2 *Make the mocktail:* Fill a cocktail mixing glass with ice. Add 1 ounce of the simple syrup and the lemon and lime juices, then stir. Gently stir in the seltzer and luster dust. Strain into two cocktail coupes or martini glasses. Store leftover syrup in an airtight container in the fridge for up to 2 weeks.

COOK'S NOTE: Due to the Yetitini's vibrant color, it's been known to stain clothing. Use extra caution if you're wearing white.

NEVERMORE ACADEMY

o ✳ ❖ ○ ✳ ○

Parties & Events
MANUAL

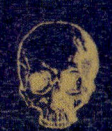     

✦○◐○✦○◐○✦○◐○✦○◐○✦○◐○✦○◐○✦○◐○✦

While we cannot possibly invite everyone to Nevermore Academy for every special occasion, we can suggest ways you normies can throw your own themed parties, inspired by our illustrious school. And so, in this spirit, we have created the following party plans for you to use as guidelines when hosting a scary soirée all your own.

On the following pages you'll find suggestions for décor, proper dress, and, of course, food and drinks for several possible events. Whether you want to throw your own Rave'N Ball (see page 206), invite friends over for a Freaksgiving Feast (see page 210), have a date night in as romantic as Morticia and Gomez's (see page 214), or even host your own Secret Society Social (see page 212)—or a watch party for your favorite show—these plans are guaranteed to make your party particularly peculiar.

✦○◐○✦○◐○✦○◐○✦○◐○✦○◐○✦○◐○✦○◐○✦

The Rave'N Ball

The Rave'N Ball is a long-standing Nevermore Academy tradition, held yearly. While it's not compulsory to attend, most students enjoy dressing up and dancing to our DJ who spins the latest pop songs along with the goth classics. Each student is allowed to invite a date, and it's not required that these guests attend Nevermore Academy themselves. At the dance, we offer students a variety of appetizers, desserts, and drinks to be enjoyed when taking a break from getting their "goo-goo-muck" on.

✷ DÉCOR IDEAS ✷

Theming is very important at the Rave'N Ball, and we advise you to pick your premise with care. No one wants to attend a party that gives off "Halloween pop-up store threw up in your living room" vibes. Be clear on your theme from the start, and keep it in mind when you select your music, décor, food, and attire.

In 1990 we threw a **GOTH AND GLAMOUR** event (which came to a tragic end due to the untimely death of Garrett Gates—though to be fair, murder and mayhem did go along nicely with the theme). If you want to throw your own goth ball, lean into everything being black or red. Envision black velvet tablecloths, elaborate candelabras with blood-red candles, old-fashioned goblets by a punch bowl giving off dry ice smoke (see page 199). Consider stringing faux spiderwebs here and there to really push the creepy old mansion feel.

Alternately, if your theme is **CLIMATE CRISIS MEETS EXTINCTION EVENT**, you'll want brighter blues and whites to evoke our rapidly evaporating oceans and tragically melting glaciers. But in a fun way!

Whatever you choose, make sure your theme is properly announced beforehand in beautiful handwritten invitations delivered to invitees' doors. Encourage guests to dress thematically. Rolling up to a goth party in a blow-up dinosaur disguise can be a real buzzkill (unless your theme happens to be Extinction, in which case this costume would fit in quite well).

SHOPPING LIST
✷ GOTH AND GLAMOUR ✷

- *black velvet tablecloths*
- *elaborate candelabras*

- *old-fashioned goblets & punch bowl*
- *dry ice*

- *faux spiderwebs*
- *blood-red candles*

✦ FOOD & DRINK ✦

At this type of party, everyone wants to graze between dances rather than sit down for an entire meal. We recommend you offer mostly finger foods that are easy to walk around with on a plate without accidentally spilling anything on your date. Our Soul-Sucking Salsa & Chips, Blackened Buffalo Bat Wings, and Mummified Brie with crackers are all good choices.

IF YOU'RE CELEBRATING SOMETHING SPECIAL, you might want to serve a signature cake to mark the occasion. The cake can vary, based on your theme. The Rave to the Grave Cake is perfect for any Halloween-themed soirée. If you'd rather offer single-serving desserts, you might try Sirens in the Black Sea or Bleeding Heart Cake.

LASTLY, NO PARTY IS COMPLETE WITHOUT DRINKS. We like to offer a signature mocktail like the Yetitini to match our ball's yearly theme. If you have an Under the Sea–themed event, you might serve the Undersea Pearl Tea. If you're vamping it up, we'd suggest serving the Bloody Mary. If you can't decide, perhaps pair the Make It Black! and Make It Pink! drinks, filling two side-by-side punch bowls and letting guests vote with their cups.

NOTE: Be aware we've had some unfortunate incidents in the past where one or more of our delinquent students have taken it upon themselves to spike the punch bowl. We would suggest recruiting a volunteer to keep an eye on the drinks table at all times if you don't want to take a chance. Also, monitoring all entrances to the party is essential to avoid any vengeful normies crashing your soirée and dousing your guests in pig's blood (or red paint if they're too cheap to spring for the good stuff).

SUGGESTED MENU

Snacks

Soul-Sucking Salsa
& Chips 48

Blackened Buffalo
Bat Wings 56

Mummified Brie *with*
crackers 60

Desserts

Rave to the Grave Cake
145

Sirens in the Black Sea 151

Bleeding Heart Cake
142

Beverages

Yetitini 200

Undersea Pearl Tea 194

Bloody Mary 180

Make It Black! 176 *and*
Make It Pink! 179

"WHEN THE DANCE FLOOR CALLS,
YOU GOTTA ANSWER."
—Eugene Ottinger

THE RAVE'N BALL

Freaksgiving Feast

You've heard of Thanksgiving and you may have even heard of Friendsgiving. But you've never experienced this unique Nevermore Academy twist on a holiday feast we've lovingly dubbed Freaksgiving. Started by a group of students in the early 1800s after a freak snowstorm stranded them at school for the holidays, it's now become an academy tradition. Modeled after a traditional American Thanksgiving meal of turkey with all the trimmings, the menu has been tweaked by our chefs to make it creepier and kookier, just like our student body. Perfect for freaking out the family when it's your turn to hold the annual feast. We promise the look of horror on Aunt Edna's face will make it all worthwhile.

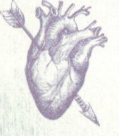

✦ DÉCOR IDEAS ✦

Shake things up at your traditional Thanksgiving table by giving it a morbid makeover. Start with a black tablecloth, then add plastic skulls, mini pumpkins, and colorful gourds, all draped in thick fake spiderwebs to give the table a freaky, autumnal feel.

BEFORE YOUR GUESTS ARRIVE, turn off all electric lamps and light the room with gothic candelabras, which will cast flickering shadows throughout dinner, making the food look even creepier. If you have room, consider placing a skeletal "guest" to sit at the head of the table, dressed in his gothic best. (If someone asks, look confused and pretend you can't see him.)

FOR ATMOSPHERE, skip any monster mashing and stream soft, haunting classical music instead. And forget asking your guests what they're thankful for at the start of the meal—we all know how boring that can be! Instead, ask them what scares them the most—and file that intel away to use when hosting next year's event!

SHOPPING LIST

- *black tablecloth*
- *plastic skulls*
- *mini pumpkins*
- *colorful gourds*
- *fake spiderwebs*
- *LED ice cubes*

✦ FOOD & DRINK ✦

Just like the traditional Thanksgiving feast, this is a full sit-down meal with a main course of turkey accompanied by all the trimmings, desserts, and drinks. You can also whip up some of our finger food appetizers and sinister sips to keep your guests happy while the main meal is being prepared.

THE MAIN COURSE, Blood-Glazed Turkey Breast, is made with just the breast of the turkey rather than the entire bird, which will save hours in preparation time. If you have any vegetarians coming to dinner, you might pair it with Uncle Fester's Famous Brain Roast, which is, contrary to its name, 100 percent brain-free and made from cauliflower.

FOR SIDES, we suggest our Blood Orange Cranberry Sauce and Edgar Allan Poe'tatoes—Nevermore Academy's twist on the classics for guests who like both sweet and salty sides. And you can try your hand at Thing's Pumpkin Pinkies—otherwise known as candied pumpkin, a traditional Mexican Day of the Dead sweet.

FOR DESSERT, you have the choice of going traditional with the As Jericho as Apple Pie, harking back to the days of old, or you can stick to the theme and serve the Rave to the Grave Cake decorated with Headstones of Horrors and Goody's Ghost.

TO DRINK, we suggest Wednesday Addams's favorite Make It Black! mocktail and Yoko Tanaka's Bloody Mary, served in clear glasses to maximize their black or red hue. You might also consider purchasing LED ice cubes to drop in each drink to give them a gory glow.

SUGGESTED MENU

Entrées

Blood-Glazed Turkey Breast
113

Uncle Fester's Famous
Brain Roast
128

Sides

Blood Orange Cranberry Sauce
114

Edgar Allan Poe'tatoes
117

Thing's Pumpkin Pinkies
157

Desserts

As Jericho as Apple Pie
167

Rave to the Grave Cake 145
with Headstones of Horrors 148
and Goody's Ghost 170

Beverages

Make It Black!
176

Bloody Mary
180

Secret Society Social

It's no secret that the Nightshade Society is an elite club, which means our membership demands the best of the best. We try to provide that during our midnight meetings in the Nevermore Academy secret library, serving up tasty apps and delicious drinks, all carefully curated based on our members' unique backgrounds and tastes. And while you, as a normie, will likely never get an invitation to join our exclusive society (sorry, we don't make the rules!), you could consider throwing your own midnight meeting or just serving bites at your next watch party in our honor. Just beware, some of these recipes are a bit . . . wild . . . just like the members of our group. Don't blame us if you're suddenly skinny-dipping without a care.

✷ DÉCOR IDEAS ✷

THINK SECRET LIBRARY VIBES! Find some old but inexpensive tomes from a used bookstore to decorate your shelves. Dim the lamps and light candles around the room. You'll need a table for the food and drinks; we suggest placing it against the wall so there's enough room to form a circle for any ceremonies you might like to hold during your meeting. Also, we advise you to keep some extra rope, a blindfold, and a gag on hand, just in case a nosy someone tries to infiltrate your event and you need to take care of them.

IN THE MEANTIME, have your guests arrive in theme, wearing purple hooded cloaks and Venetian-style masks, available at most party stores or costume shops. And come up with a riddle for them to solve or a secret snap they need to do before they're allowed through the front door.

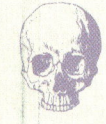

SHOPPING LIST

- used books
- candles

- rope
- blindfold & gag

- purple hooded cloaks
- Venetian masks

✴ FOOD & DRINK ✴

Since this is not a sit-down event, we suggest serving finger foods and drinks that are easy to walk around with. Offer a good variety to appeal to all tastes. We like the Full-Moon Franks for our Furs, the Blackened Buffalo Bat Wings for our Fangs, Mummified Brie for our Stoners, and Siren Salmon & Seaweed Toast for our Scales.

YOU MIGHT ALSO TRY Wednesday's Soul-Sucking Salsa & Chips, which has proven a crowd favorite, even though the recipe's creator refused to accept her invitation to our club. And no Nightshade Society meeting would be complete without our signature dessert, Nightshade Society Poe Parfait, made with sweet layers that match our purple and black uniforms.

MOCKTAILS are also a must at these parties. Our signature drink, created by our amateur mixologist Yoko Tanaka, is the Nightshade Society Nightcap, made with cinnamon and forbidden rice. You can also serve Undersea Pearl Tea (perfect for Scales!), a Bloody Mary (beloved by Fangs), or even a Stone Cold Brew (a caffeine kick for Stoners).

Morticia and Gomez's Date Night In

While Gomez and I do love going out on the town and dancing till dawn, sometimes we just want to stay home and relax by a roaring fire. Let's face it, there's nothing more romantic than making a meal together, then sitting down at a beautiful candlelit table—just the two of you—to taste the fruits of your labor. There are no condescending waiters. No orders gotten wrong. No annoying families at the next table with their screaming, whining, chicken-nugget-chowing children. Just you and your loved one, sharing your dark secrets and making plans for the future. You'll realize romance is not dead (unless, by chance, you want it to be . . .).

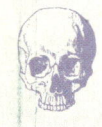

✳ DÉCOR IDEAS ✳

The décor for a date night is entirely up to you. Since you don't have to worry about what others will think or post on their social media pages the next day, you are free to theme things however you desire. Maybe you want to set an elegant gothic table, complete with candles and skulls and lace. Or maybe you want to feed each other finger foods in front of the fire. And then, of course, there's our favorite—treating yourself to treats in your home torture chamber. Honestly, it's all up to you—Gomez and I won't judge!

SHOPPING LIST

- gothic table
- fireplace
- home torture chamber
- skulls & lace
- candles

✶ FOOD & DRINK ✶

What we love most about a date night in is we're able to re-create our favorite recipes without being limited to someone else's menu. I usually like to start with my special Eyeball Soup, to let Gomez know I have eyes only for him. In turn, he loves making Black Heart Chicken Breast for our main course, which uses a chocolaty mole sauce as dark and delicious as our love. And maybe we'll add some Frightening Fajitas as well. To complete the meal, I suggest Boil Them in Oil Rice and Paint It Black Beans.

Though Gomez is the only dessert I really need, sometimes we do enjoy something extra sweet, like Bleeding Heart Cake. You can stab it with your fork and watch the blood flow out onto your plate, a beautiful reminder of how love and death are intertwined. Pair it with my Mija's Mud, a thick, rich hot chocolate sure to complete the experience.

SUGGESTED MENU

Starter

Eyeball Soup
123

Entrées

Black Heart Chicken Breast
109

Frightening Fajitas
96

Sides

Boil Them in Oil Rice
127

Paint It Black Beans
84

Dessert

Bleeding Heart Cake
142

Beverage

Mija's Mud
188

Fun Wednesday Facts

- While Nevermore Academy is said to be in Vermont, the exterior building is actually Cantacuzino Castle, located in Romania, where the series was filmed. And while the town of Jericho, Vermont, is a real place, the show's creators reimagined it and built the set at the Bucharest Film Studios of Buftea, also in Romania.

- Thing is not computer generated but is played by actor-magician Victor Dorobantu, who wore a full-coverage blue suit so his body could be edited out later.

- Actress Jenna Ortega learned to play the cello for her role as Wednesday. She also learned to fence.

- Wednesday never blinks once in the entire show.

- There are multiple references to Edgar Allan Poe in the series, among them: The school's name, Nevermore Academy, is an ode to his poem "The Raven." During the eponymous Poe Cup, Wednesday and Enid's team pays homage to Poe's short story "The Black Cat." The Rave'N Ball is another reference to his poem, and the Nightshade Society is a nod to his short story "Morella," which is another name for the nightshade plant.

Resources

✦◇✦◇✦◇✦◇✦◇✦◇✦◇✦◇✦◇✦◇✦◇✦◇✦◇✦◇✦◇✦◇✦◇✦◇✦◇✦

BLACK SESAME PASTE This paste can be found in Asian markets, some grocery stores, and online. You can also make it yourself using black sesame seeds and a good food processor: Simply grind 1 cup of seeds in the food processor until the seeds release their natural oils and the mixture turns into a smooth, glossy paste. If buying premade paste, make sure that black sesame seeds are the only ingredient listed.

CHILES Dried guajillo, pasilla, and mulato chiles can be found in many Latin American markets, specialty spice shops, some grocery stores, and online. Calabrian chiles are usually found jarred in oil.

FREEZE-DRIED FRUIT POWDERS These are powders made of freeze-dried fruits that impart strong fruit flavors without adding moisture to a dish or using artificial extracts or flavorings. They can be found in some grocery stores, health food stores, and online. You might also find them in large department stores and some big-box stores. Pulse these powders in a food processor until finely ground.

HEADSTONE-SHAPED COOKIE CUTTERS Keep an eye out for these fun kitchen tools in big-box stores, craft stores, and other shops where baking supplies are sold during Halloween. Otherwise, they are typically found year-round online.

LUSTER AND PETAL DUST These are powdered pigments used to add color to drinks, desserts, and other dishes. Luster dust is typically metallic in appearance and adds a glittery or shimmering effect, in addition to color. Petal dust is pure pigment with a matte finish. Both can be found in specialty baking supply shops, some craft stores, and online.

MEXICAN OREGANO Although widely accepted as a type of oregano, Mexican oregano is actually in a different family of plants. Mediterranean oregano is in the mint family, whereas Mexican oregano is in the verbena family. The latter has some similar aromas to Mediterranean oregano, but it is more floral and citrusy. If you can't find Mexican oregano, marjoram is a better substitute than Mediterranean oregano.

RUBY CHOCOLATE Made from ruby cocoa beans and introduced to the market in 2017 by Barry Callebaut, this variety of chocolate boasts a pink, sometimes purple, color. In addition to its unique color, this chocolate has a sweet, slightly sour and acidic taste with rich, fruity flavor. It can be found in many grocery stores and online.

UBE Ube is a purple yam originally from the Philippines. Though similar to a purple sweet potato, it's sweeter with a mellower taste. Because of its slightly nutty vanilla flavor, it is popularly used in desserts in Filipino cuisine. Ube extract can be found in some grocery stores, Asian markets, and online.

UNSWEETENED TARO POWDER Taro powder is easily found online but can also be substituted with purple sweet potato powder—they are different plants but taste similar.

✦◇✦◇✦◇✦◇✦◇✦◇✦◇✦◇✦◇✦◇✦◇✦◇✦◇✦◇✦◇✦◇✦◇✦◇✦◇✦

Index

About the Authors

MARI MANCUSI regrets having never applied to Nevermore Academy, as she's certain she'd have fit right in. An Emmy-winning former television producer and author of more than thirty books—including *The Nightmare Before Christmas* Twisted Tale from Disney Press—she has always been a huge Tim Burton fan and has streamed *Wednesday* more times than Thing has fingers. When not writing, she enjoys going to Disney World, playing video games, and watching scary (and cheesy!) horror movies.

JARRETT MELENDEZ is an award-winning comic book writer, cookbook author, and food journalist. His work has appeared in *Bon Appétit, Saveur, Epicurious,* and Food52, and he is the author of *My Pokémon Baking Book and RuneScape: The Official Cookbook.* His best-known work is *Chef's Kiss* from Oni Press, which won the Alex Award from the American Library Association and was nominated for both a GLAAD award for Outstanding Graphic Novel and an Eisner Award for Best Publication for Teens.

Melendez grew up on the mean, deer-infested streets of Bucksport, Maine, but now lives in Massachusetts with his collection of Monokuro Boo plush pigs.